Palmolive Co v. Conway U.S. Supreme Court Transcript of Record with Supporting Pleadings

LOUIS QUARLES, JOHN W REYNOLDS

Palmolive Co v. Conway

Petition / LOUIS QUARLES / 1932 / 62 / 287 U.S. 601 / 53 S.Ct. 8 / 77 L.Ed. 524 / 5-9-1932
Palmolive Co v. Conway
Respondent's Brief (P) / JOHN W REYNOLDS / 1932 / 62 / 287 U.S. 601 / 53 S.Ct. 8 / 77 L.Ed. 524 / 5-31-1932

Palmolive Co v. Conway U.S. Supreme Court
Transcript of Record with Supporting Pleadings

Table of Contents

In The
SUPREME COURT OF THE UNITED STATES
October Term, 1931.

No. 920   62

THE PALMOLIVE COMPANY, a Delaware corporation,

Petitioner and Appellant Below,

vs.

W. J. CONWAY, CHARLES D. ROSA, EDWARD L. KELLEY, as Members of the Wisconsin Tax Commission, and PATRICK McMANUS, as Treasurer of Milwaukee County,

Respondents and Appellees Below.

Petition for Writ of Certiorari
to the United States Circuit Court of Appeals
for the Seventh Circuit
and
Brief in Support Thereof.

LOUIS QUARLES,
and
HARRY L. BUTLER,
Counsel for Petitioner.

SUBJECT INDEX OF MATTER IN PETITION AND BRIEF.

Argument—*Continued.*

TABLE OF CASES.

Table of Cases—*Continued.*

TABLE OF STATUTES.

In The
SUPREME COURT OF THE UNITED STATES
October Term, 1931.

No. ----------

THE PALMOLIVE COMPANY, a Delaware corporation,

Petitioner and Appellant Below,

vs.

W. J. CONWAY, CHARLES D. ROSA, EDWARD L.
KELLEY, as Members of the Wisconsin Tax Commission,
and PATRICK McMANUS, as Treasurer of Milwaukee
County,

Respondents and Appellees Below.

Petition for Writ of Certiorari

To the Honorable, the Chief Justice and the Associate Justices of the Supreme Court of the United States:

Your petitioner respectfully shows:

I.   Summary Statement of the Matter Involved.

This is a suit in equity to restrain the collection of income taxes reassessed in 1928 by the Wisconsin Tax Commission on the 1924, 1925 and 1926 incomes of The Palmolive Company, a Wisconsin corporation, herein called the taxpayer.

Plaintiff, The Palmolive Company of Delaware, (which, before change of name in 1927, was Western Operating Company) is the party in interest in virtue of the later dissolution of the taxpayer in 1927 and of the distribution of its assets to plaintiff as stockholder.

The jurisdiction is rested on denial of due process and diversity of citizenship.

The issues embrace the questions:

(1) Whether the statutory formula by which income was determined, and the resulting reassessment, operated to subject the taxpayer to taxation upon a large amount of income derived and realized outside Wisconsin.

(2) Whether the Commission acted without statutory authority and beyond its jurisdicton in applying the statutory formula to this case.

By decree of date October 9, 1930, the District Court for the Western District of Wisconsin (Honorable Walter C. Lindley presiding) affirmed the reassessment, except in a minor particular not here material. His opinion is at 577-588 R. and is reported

> *Palmolive Company vs. Conway,* 43 Fed. (2d) 226.

The Court of Appeals (7th Circuit) affirmed the District Court. Opinion (by Honorable Samuel Alschuler, C. J.) of date February 13, 1932, R. 610, reported 56 Fed. (2d) 83.

The taxpayer made return to defendant, Wisconsn Tax Commission, of its taxable income for the above income years, and paid taxes in accordance with such returns. The aggregate taxable income thus returned was $913,787. The aggregate tax paid was $61,885 (R. 182, 230, 231, 241, 245, 246, 252, 289, 304).

In 1927, the Commission made an audit, not only of the separate books and accounts of the taxpayer, but of three other related and commonly controlled corporations, i. e. The Palmolive Company, of Delaware, herein called National Company, (which later became Palmolive-Peet Company and later Colgate-Palmolive-Peet Company), Buckingham Agency of Illinois, and Western Operating Company (the plaintiff) (R. 308, 341). The two companies first named transacted no business in Wisconsin.

Following such audit, the Commission reassessed the income of the taxpayer for the tax years by treating the four companies as one, and applying to their combined apportionment income a statutory formula (Sec. 71.02 (3)(d)) which measured income according to the arithmetical average of the ratios of (1) Wisconsin property, (2) Wisconsin sales, (3) Wisconsin manufacturing cost, to the respective totals of each of such items.

The formula produced an aggregate reassessment of $4,023,826 and a resulting tax of $281,070 (R. 320). The taxable income returned by the taxpayer was thus quadrupled.

For many years prior to 1924 the taxpayer had manufactured soap products at its domicile at Milwaukee and marketed them throughout the country, and to some extent in foreign countries, principally under the registered trade name "Palmolive."

The related corporations were organized in 1923, pursuant to the determination of the directors and stockholders of the old Company (taxpayer) to rearrange and relocate the former business, transfer all property and assets (including trade name and good will) to the National Company except certain property located in Wisconsin, namely the factory and equipment and merchandise inventories at Milwaukee and such accounts receivable as had arisen from marketing in Wisconsin alone, and to confine the future business of the old Company (taxpayer) to the output manufacture of soap products at the factory, the marketing in Wisconsin of such portion thereof as should be required to meet the demands of Wisconsin trade, and the wholesale of the remainder of the output to the National Company to be by it marketed along with the output of a smaller factory in another state and of additional outside factories in contemplation.

As a part of the reorganization plan the title to the factory and equipment was to go to plaintiff (then Western Operating Company) which in turn was to lease the same to the taxpayer, the plaintiff transacting no other business.

Such rearrangement of situs and division of former activities, and limitation of Wisconsin activities, was consummated and became effective at the end of 1923, since which time, and throughout the tax years, the Wisconsin business was thus limited, and all other business, including all domestic and foreign marketing business (except the supplying of the Wisconsin trade by the taxpayer), has been independently conducted by the National Company, located at Chicago (R. 21, 23, 25-28, 33, 38-39).

The above rearrangement of the former business was prompted by considerations of economy, and by plans of expansion, largely through contemplated mergers (later consummated) which were contingent on such removal to a large financial and distributing center. The record does not indicate, but in view of Wisconsin tax burdens it should go without saying that tax economy was not overlooked (R. 23, 26-27).

The taxpayer's returns were made on the basis of its separate books of account, which in turn reflected all profits from marketing in Wisconsin, and all profits from manufacture and wholesale to National Company of remaining factory output under certain cost plus contracts with the latter, one for the year 1924 and another covering the two succeeding years (R. 28, 84, 219, 395).

The 1924 contract provided for a profit to the taxpayer of 3% over cost of manufacture, the subsequent contract for 6% over factory cost. In the accounting (on the basis of which 1924 income was returned) the proceeds derived by the taxpayer from sales of the by-product, glycerine, were, through error, not deducted from cost of materials in arriving at factory cost, as should have been done (according to uniformly accepted trade practice), and no interest was credited on advances made by the National Company (R. 29). By reason of this, the contract yield for 1924 was greater than it would have been had the profit percentage been 6% instead of 3% (R. 50). In consequence, the taxable income as returned by the taxpayer for the three years was somewhat larger than would have been yielded by the payment to the taxpayer of factory cost, after glycerine deduction, plus 6%.

Pursuant to statute, a hearing was had as to the propriety of the Commission reassessment. Conceding it to be the right and duty of the Commission to scrutinize the inter-company cost plus contracts, the taxpayer adduced evidence showing that a profit of 6% of factory cost (after credit for glycerine sales) was the maximum of fair and reasonable profit derivable from the business of manufacturing and wholesaling to a stranger who marketed the product, that contracts of that character were common in the business, that such manufacture and wholesale was practically a non-risk business of assured return, and that, assuming efficient management, skillful advertising and efficient sales organization, the marketing business, in common trade practice, yielded the much larger profit (R. 37, 42-44, 62-63, 65, 67).

Following the hearing the Commission confirmed its reassessment, thereby finally imposing on the taxpayer an added tax on about $3,000,000 of additional income.

The basic ground on which the Court of Appeals (as well as the District Court) sustained the reassessment was this:

(1) There was impressed upon the manufacturing business of the taxpayer, and Wisconsin was entitled to share to some undefined extent in, income arising from good name and good will created in former years, wherefore, "a reasonable profit attributable to this manufacturing function cannot be adequately measured by a percentage of the cost of material and labor and the like." The effect of this ruling was in substance to exclude as immaterial and deny effect to the evidence in the record as to the fairness and adequacy of the income yielded by the contracts.

(2) A secondary and supporting judicial justification for the Commission reassessment was this: The parties to the contracts had not included in manufacturing cost (and hence in the base to which was applied the contractual percentage) certain items of general or overhead expense which, in the judicial view, should have been included, that the profit percentage was inadequate, and that credit should have been given on account of sales of the by-product glycerine. Without attempt to designate by figures the extent to which the respective changes would affect income the court concluded that "the record does not admit of estimates better or closer than those which the Tax Commission made."

(3) Incidentally and finally the Court declared that the taxpayer fell "far short of its statutory duty of making 'a true and accurate statement of its taxable Wisconsin income.'"

II. Reasons Relied on for Allowance of Writ.

The ruling of the Court of Appeals (as well as that of the District Court) contravenes important and fundamental rights of plaintiff, denies due process, conflicts with applicable decisions of this Court, and of the Wisconsin and other courts, departs from the accepted and usual course of judicial proceeding, and presents questions vitally affecting the constitutional exercise by the different states of taxing power and jurisdiction, in that the decision:

(a) Sanctions Commission interference with the exercise by a Wisconsin taxpayer of the lawful right to reorganize a unitary business by removing a distinct and separate part of it to another state and there conducting it through a separate corporate entity. Under the decision it is not enough that the taxpayer proves by evidence that it has returned and paid the income actually derived or fairly derivable from the limited business left in the state. The tax authorities are in effect justified in ruling that such evidence proves nothing because, as asserted, some hypothetical and unmeasurable part of the good will of the former unitary business inheres in the manufacturing activities left in Wisconsin, whether income therefrom is realized there or realized (as the evidence shows) from out-of-state marketing business.

Thus Wisconsin, with the approval of the lower court, is permitted to set up the barrier of double taxation against exercise by the owner of the right to remove to another state and there conduct through a separate corporate entity an independent part of a former unitary business. By arbitrary tax exaction the owner, if he would remove at all, must dismantle his Wisconsin plant and remove entirely.

(b) Sanctions the exaction from the taxpayer (against the evidence and notwithstanding the Wisconsin statute expressly limits taxable income to that "derived from property located and business transacted within the state, Sec.

71.01''), of a tax upon income many times that shown by undisputed evidence to have been derived or reasonably or fairly derivable from business of the character and scope of that transacted in Wisconsin, thereby burdening the tax-payer with taxes on millions of income derived and realized by the National Company from marketing business wholly transacted without the state.

(c)   Failed properly to interpret and to follow the decision of this Court in

> *Hans Rees' Sons Co. vs. North Carolina,* 283 U. S. 123; s. c. *Maxwell Commissioner vs. Hans Rees' Sons Co.,* 153 S. E. 850, 854.

which case in effect rules, as we submit:

(1)   That unitary characteristics of a manufacturing and marketing business do not warrant the use by the taxing authorities of the state of manufacture of an apportionment formula producing a much larger income within the state than the income indicated by evidence of similar nature to that presented (and in substance rejected) in the present case.

(2)   That the apportionment formula may not be justified on the theory that the manufacturing state may share in marketing income of the same corporation earned and realized in another state and there (as must be inferred), indirectly enhanced by good will.

(d)   Failed properly to apply and to follow the decision of the Wisconsin Supreme Court in

> *Standard Oil Company vs. Wisconsin Tax Comm.,* 197 Wis. 630; 223 N. W. 85.

which in effect rules:

(1) That where income from marketing in Wisconsin is separately shown or is separately ascertainable, the Commission may not measure income by the statutory formula here in question.

(2) That the use of the formula may not be justified upon the theory that manufacturing profits in other states are increased because the volume of Wisconsin sales contributes to the continuity and volume of the outside manufacturing operation.

(3) That taxable income should be limited to that shown· by the separate accounting to have been actually derived from sales in Wisconsin, thereby excluding alleged producing and manufacturing income derived in other states, and also excluding Wisconsin participation in good will save to the extent that it was reflected in the income derived from Wisconsin sales. In the present case the taxpayer's returns similarly reflected all income from marketing in Wisconsin.

(e) Reconstructed the terms of the inter-company contracts by substituting judicial estimate of cost of manufacture, of treatment of glycerine sales, and of profit percentage, all in contravention of universally accepted accounting and trade practice and in conflict with the evidence of record; thereby invading fundamental right and accepted course of judicial procedure and disregarding the rule that administrative action without or against evidence is arbitrary and unlawful.

Northern Pacific vs. Department of Public Works,
268 U. S. 39, 44, 45.

(f) Overlooked Section 71.14 of Wisconsin Statutes, which applies to full disclosure as precedent to judicial relief, and, instead, applied and misinterpreted Section 71.09 (3) which has no relation thereto; and disregarded the undisputed evidence that fair and full disclosure was made by the taxpayer,—a fact never questioned until the statement of the Court of Appeals above referred to.

(g)   Gave no apparent consideration to the issue that Sections 71.02 (3) (d), and 71.25 (1), Wisconsin Statutes, exclude the application to this case of the statutory formula, and that Section 71.25 recognizes the prima facie validity of operating contracts between affiliated companies and that the Commission function in such cases is to determine the adequacy of the *measure* of the contractual income, —not to reconstruct the business or to interfere with the freedom of action of the owner as to its character or scope.

WHEREFORE, petitioner prays that a writ of certiorari issue under the seal of this Court, directed to the Circuit Court of Appeals for the 7th Circuit, commanding said court to certify and send to this Court a full and complete transcript of the record and of the proceedings of the said Circuit Court of Appeals had in the case numbered and entitled on its docket No. 4523, The Palmolive Company, a Delaware corporation, Appellant, vs. W. J. Conway, Charles D. Rosa, Edward L. Kelley, as members of the Wisconsin Tax Commission, and Patrick McManus, as Treasurer of Milwaukee County, Appellees, to the end that this cause may be reviewed and determined by this Court as provided for by the statutes of the United States; and that the judgment herein of said Circuit Court of Appeals be reversed by this Court, and for such further relief as to this Court may seem proper.

Dated May 2, 1932.

THE PALMOLIVE COMPANY,
a Delaware Corporation,
By Louis Quarles,
and
Harry L. Butler,
Counsel for Petitioner.

In The
SUPREME COURT OF THE UNITED STATES
October Term, 1931.

No. ....

THE PALMOLIVE COMPANY, a Delaware corporation,

Petitioner and Appellant Below,

vs.

W. J. CONWAY, CHARLES D. ROSA, EDWARD L. KELLEY, as Members of the Wisconsin Tax Commission, and PATRICK McMANUS, as Treasurer of Milwaukee County,

Respondents and Appellees Below.

Brief in Support of Petition for Certiorari.

The suit is one to restrain the collection of income taxes reassessed by the Tax Commission on the 1924, 1925 and 1926 incomes of The Palmolive Company, a Wisconsin corporation, herein called the taxpayer.

Plaintiff, The Palmolive Company, of Delaware, is the party in interest in virtue of the dissolution of the taxpayer, in 1927, and of the distribution to plaintiff as stockholder of its assets.

The opinions of the lower courts:

The District Court for the Western District of Wisconsin, Honorable Walter C. Lindley, presiding, affirmed the reassessment, except in a minor particular not here material.

His opinion is at 577-588 R., and is reported

> *Palmolive Company vs. Conway*, 43 Fed. (2d) 226.

The Court of Appeals (7th Circuit) affirmed the District Court. Its opinion, by Honorable Samuel Alschuler, C. J. is at R. 610. Reported 56 Fed. (2d) 83.

The grounds of jurisdiction:

The jurisdiction is rested:

(1) Upon alleged denial of due process, in that the reassessment operated to subject to Wisconsin taxation some $3,000,000 of income derived from business transacted outside the state.

(2) Upon diversity of citizenship (plaintiff being a citizen of Delaware), which broadly tenders the issue that the Commission reassessment is unauthorized by Wisconsin statutes, and that it acted without jurisdiction to the prejudice of the taxpayer.

The decree of the District Court is dated October 9, 1930 and appears at R. 588.

Statement of the case:

Prior to its dissolution and during the years 1924, 1925 and 1926, The Palmolive Company of Wisconsin (taxpayer) was transacting in Milwaukee the business of manufacturing soap products in a factory there located, selling in Wisconsin, upon its own terms, such part of the factory output as was required to meet the demands of the Wisconsin trade, and wholesaling and delivering to or upon the order of The Palmolive Company of Delaware (herein called

National Company) the remaining factory output under certain cost plus contracts hereinafter referred to. The taxpayer transacted no other business in Wisconsin or elsewhere (R. 38).

The factory and equipment was leased by the taxpayer from the plaintiff (then named Western Operating Company) a Delaware corporation, for an agreed rental. Except as lessor, that Company, during the years in question, transacted no business in Wisconsin (R. 33, 60).

Both the taxpayer and its lessor of factory and equipment were subsidiaries of the National Company, the stock of the taxpayer being owned by its lessor and the stock of the latter being owned by the National Company (R. 21). Both of these companies were organized in 1923 (R. 21).

During and prior to that year the taxpayer had been manufacturing soap products in Milwaukee, and from a small beginning had built up a large business. Its soap products, largely under the registered trademark "Palmolive," were sold throughout the country and to a considerable extent in foreign countries (R. 20).

The soap business readily divides into the two important activities of manufacturing and marketing (R. 37). It was and is common in the trade for the product to be manufactured by one and marketed by another under the latter's trade-mark or trade name (R. 37, 62-63, 65, 67). The manufacture of Palmolive soap, as of other soaps, is a comparatively simple unpatented process. Anyone is free to manufacture and sell it, and some do, though, of course, they may not market under the trade name unless so authorized (R. 37, 63, 65).

The business of manufacturing and wholesaling to a responsible purchaser involves no substantial risk of loss. The hazard attaches rather to the marketing. That involves not only credit factors but also (if sales volume is to be large) an immense expenditure for selling organizations, great and uncontrollable fluctuations in inventory and possibility of enormous losses through ineffective advertising. Persistent advertising is essential to large volume sales (R. 37, 63, 64).

For the above reasons the customary manufacturing profit is very much less than the necessary marketing profit. To cost of manufacturing must be added a gross profit adequate to cover marketing costs and profit, including costs of advertising and selling and losses incident thereto (R 42, 43-44).

During 1923 the directors determined upon a reorganization and relocation of the property and business of the old Company. This was prompted by expansion plans which were to be largely achieved by mergers with other companies, then under discussion and later consummated (R. 23, 26-27).

Important economies were to be gained by transferring the old business to Chicago and the expansion and merger program was contingent on its removal there (R. 26-27). The Record does not directly show, but no doubt the fact is that Wisconsin's heavy tax burden was an additional consideration.

So it was determined to transfer to the National Company all property of the old Company, excepting factory and equipment, which was to go to plaintiff, and except raw materials, etc. at the factory, and accounts receivable which had arisen from previous sales in Wisconsin. These latter were to be left to the old Company (taxpayer). The National Company, located at Chicago, was to own and conduct all business except the leasing (by plaintiff) to the taxpayer of the Milwaukee plant and equipment and except the conducting (by the taxpayer) of the limited business of manufacturing, marketing the product in Wisconsin alone, and sale and delivery of remaining output to the National Company (R. 21, 23, 26-27, 33, 38, 39).

The reorganization, removal and transfers contemplated by the plan were fully consummated during and became effective at the end of the year 1923 (R. 21).

The transfer to the National Company included a factory in another state, a factory site in another, all outside inventories, accounts, property connected with the many sales agencies over the country, trademarks, good will, and all other property save the factory, inventories and local accounts left in Wisconsin. Extensive offices were established in Chicago. All personnel, except that required for the limited business to be transacted in Milwaukee, was moved to Chicago (R. 25).

Since the beginning of 1924 the three corporations have transacted business as separate corporate entities (though commonly owned), separate books of account have been kept, and the business of the taxpayer (as well as of its lessor) has been limited to that contemplated by the reorganization plan (R. 28, 38).

The taxable income return by the taxpayer for each of the years 1924, 1925 and 1926, based on its separate books of account, together with the tax for each year (which in due course was paid by the taxpayer) are as follows (R. 182, 230, 231, 241, 245, 246, 252, 289, 304):

Year	Taxable Income Returned	Tax Paid
1924	$298,219.97	$20,676.23
1925	$273,781.48	$18,965.50
1926	$341,786.18	$22,243.18
Totals	$913,787.63	$61,884.91

In 1927 the Commission audited the books and accounts of all three companies (and also of Buckingham Agency, not here material). Following such audit, it ignored the separate corporate entities, treated all property and business as though owned and conducted by the National Company, and determined taxable income of the taxpayer by applying the apportionment formula provided in Section 71.02 (3) (d) Wisconsin Stats., i. e., the application to combined net incomes of the four companies (less certain statutory deductions not here material), of an apportionment factor consisting of the arithmetical average of three percentages, (1) of Wisconsin property, (2) of cost of manufacturing in Wisconsin, and (3) of sales in Wisconsin, to the respective totals of those items everywhere.

The resulting reassessed income for each of the tax years and the tax thereon are as follows:

Year	Income as Re-Assessed	Resulting Tax
1924	$1,297,967.80	$90,658.59
1925	$1,357,978.74	$94,859.36
1926	$1,367,879.96	$95,552.43
Totals	$4,023,826.50	$281,070.38

Thus the apportionment method applied by the Commission operated to more than quadruple the taxable income actually derived from the business actually transacted by the taxpayer.

Pursuant to statute, the plaintiff (successor in interest of the taxpayer) protested the Commission reassessment, and was accorded a statutory hearing at which we presented evidence hereinafter referred to.

It was conceded by the Commission auditor that the income returned by the taxpayer for each of the three years truly reflected the income as shown by its separate books and accounts (R. 84). Also that the books and accounts reflected the income yielded by the sale of the product to the Wisconsin trade and also that yielded from wholesale manufacture and delivery under the cost plus contracts (R. 84).

There were two of these contracts, one operative during 1924 and the other operative during 1925 and 1926. The 1924 contract provided for payment to the taxpayer of "cost of manufacture" plus 3% (R. 220). The contract for subsequent years provided for the payment of "factory cost" plus 6%, and the term factory cost was defined (R. 396). The latter contract also provided that the National Company should make advances to the taxpayer for raw materials, etc., the same to carry interest at 5½% (R. 396, 397). This latter provision was not embraced in the 1924 contract.

In arriving at "cost of manufacture," or its equivalent "factory cost," it was standard accounting practice, uniformly understood and accepted in the trade, to reduce the cost of material by the proceeds derived by the manufacturer from the sale (in its crude state) of the by-product glycerine (R. 105, 129, 130, 148, 154). The price of gylcerine is greatly affected by foreign quotations and varies a great deal. The sale proceeds for the three years were, respectively, $493,842, $668,049 and $939,765 (R. 48, 348). At the time of the hearing it was back to its 1924 price (R. 51). Factory cost after glycerine deduction averaged around $10,574,000 (R. 183, 230, 245, 49). It is obvious that the trade practice of deducting glycerine from manufacturing cost assures the manufacturer a more stable return since he is relieved of the risk of market fluctuations.

Through accounting error in 1924, the taxpayer made no deduction from factory cost for the amount received by it from that year's glycerine sales. The discovery of this, at the end of the year, apparently led to two changes, i. e., the *accounting* was changed to thereafter reflect glycerine deduction and interest credit on advancements from the National Company, and the *contract* was changed by raising the percentage over factory cost from 3% to 6% and by providing for the interest credit. The erroneous accounting for 1924 was, however, left unchanged, though the omission of the glycerine deduction operated to give a larger profit for that year (and hence a larger taxable income) than would have been yielded by a 6% rate with glycerine deduction (R. 29, C. 48-50).

Much has been made of the testimony of Mr. Lansing (secretary and comptroller of the National Company) that it was "too much clerical work to go back" and change the erroneous 1924 accounting, but it is very apparent from his immediately succeeding testimony that the year's operation had led the parties to believe that the taxpayer should receive more than 3% after glycerine deduction, and that a fair and adequate yield would be reflected by 6%, after such deduction and with interest credit (R. 48-50).

Before recurring to the testimony, it is also pertinent to note the misconception involved in the statement of the trial court to the effect that it was plaintiff's insistence "that such a contract between two such distinct entities as two corporations must be accepted at its face value, and that to ignore or go behind such contracts is to interfere with the constitutional rights of the parties to contract" (R. 583).

At no time has any such contention been made. It has been conceded throughout that the inter-company relationship not only authorized, but made it the duty of, the Commission to look behind the contracts.

9

What plaintiff has insisted on is this: that in looking behind the contracts, the Commission was without constitutional or statutory authority to reconstruct the character and scope of the restricted business which the parties of lawful right had determined to transact in Wisconsin, and that its inquiry was limited to the fair yield from *that* business without inclusion of marketing income realized by another corporation in another state, and, moreover, that it was bound to determine the inquiry in accord with and not in disregard of the evidence.

The testimony as to fairness of contract yield:

The testimony clearly disclosed that it was common practice for a soap manufacturer to manufacture and deliver soap to another on a cost plus basis, to be marketed by the latter under his own brand. Soap thus manufactured is commonly known in the trade as private brand soap (R. 67).

According to the undisputed testimony the profit percentage over factory cost, after deduction for glycerine sales, is from 1% to 6%.

Mr. Lansing testified that the National Company had always manufactured private brand soap for others under cost plus contracts yielding not over 6% (R. 37).

Mr. Wrisley, Vice-president and General Manager of a competitive soap company, testified that his company and many others named by him made a practice of contracting for the "manufacture of toilet soaps or private brand soaps on a basis of manufacturing cost plus 6% or less * * * figuring cost as defined in the contracts, that is, raw materials, labor and factory burden" (R. 62, 63, 65). Between 40% and 50% of the output of his factory was sold on a cost plus basis (R. 65). His practice conformed to the standard practice of the industry in treating glycerine proceeds as a reduction from raw material cost (R. 62).

Mr. Wrisley, after testifying to his familiarity with the 1924 and 1925 contracts in question, further stated that as an experienced soap manufacturer he would be willing to enter into such contracts for the manufacture of Palmolive or similar toilet soaps "because we consider it profitable business" (R. 62, 148).

From his experience in the industry, "the terms of these contracts (in question) were fair and reasonable to the company manufacturing the soap" (R. 63).

Asked whether he thought "a business that sold its entire output at cost plus 3% or 6% could prosper if it had no other customers" he answered "it certainly could as long as it had the contract" (R. 65, 151).

The Wrisley plant was considerably smaller than the Milwaukee plant, but the equipment was the same basically, and he was able to make "logical comparison between the volume produced and the cost of producing that volume" in the case of his plant and of the Milwaukee plant (R. 64).

Mr. Jones, Secretary and Sales Manager of a competitive soap company (James S. Kirk & Company) testified that for many years his Company had been producing a product identical with Palmolive soap (R. 68); that soap manufacturers are continuously entering into and operating under similar contracts (R. 67); that his Company, in accordance with standard practice, deducted glycerine sales from the cost of raw materials (R. 66); that approximately 10% of his total volume of business was conducted on cost plus contracts (R. 70).

Asked whether his business would "be a profitable enterprise if the entire business were conducted on a cost plus basis in accordance with a contract such as being discussed here, anywhere from 1%—cost plus 1% to cost plus 6%," the witness answered "yes" (R. 70, 159).

Asked whether he, as an experienced manufacturer, would "enter into contracts such as these or either of them for the manufacture of Palmolive soap or similar toilet soap," he replied "Yes, very gladly. As a matter of fact we have for years been manufacturing all the way from 6% and even 1%, and sometimes below cost on certain occasions" (R. 66, 154),—manufacture below cost being exceptional and to help take care of the overhead, his company making money on most of its contracts (R. 70, 158, 159).

After examination of the contracts he further testified that he regarded their terms as "fair and reasonable to the company manufacturing the soap" (R. 67, 155).

To the question whether the profits of his company would be as great if it was disposing of its entire production under similar contracts, he replied in the negative, explaining that his company, having valuable advertised brands which had accumulated a valuable good will in the trade-mark, was able to market the brand soap at a higher profit than on private brand sales (R. 70, 159).

This last testimony was in line with the undisputed evidence that private brand manufacture and sale carried a much lower margin of profit than did marketing under well advertised and popular trade names (R. 65).

It pointed a distinction which seems to have been ignored in the present case, namely, that the income of the taxpayer should not be measured on the basis of the larger profits realized from the marketing of trade name soap (which was *not* the business it transacted) but on the basis of manufacturing and selling private brand soap (which *was* the business transacted) and which, according to the experienced and disinterested witnesses, carried a maximum profit of 6% over factory cost after glycerine deduction.

In addition to the foregoing testimony, there were put in evidence several foreign, arm's length contracts, with a cost and profit analysis (R. 498) showing the profit to the manufacturer in terms of percentage of factory cost, after glycerine deduction, and hence, on a basis comparable with the maximum of 6% testified to by the witnesses and with the 6% of the contracts in question (the 1924 contract having yielded over 6% after glycerine deduction).

The resulting cost plus percentages were:

For 1926, in France 4.62%, in Mexico 5.69%; for 1927, in Belgium 5%, in France 4.76%, in Germany 7.37%, in Holland 4.76%, in Italy 5.73%, in Mexico 5.87%; for 1928, in Belgium 4.65%, in France 4.45%, in Germany, 7.56%, in Holland 4.46%, in Italy 6.59%, and in Mexico 5.71%. Disregarding the results of the Belgian contract (expressed in kilos) the average of these percentages of profit, based on the quantities to which applicable, was 5.3%.

Mr. Lansing testified that the percentage of profit was about the same the world over, but if anything "the American manufacturers are willing to take a smaller margin of profit than foreign manufacturers" (R. 39, 117) and that cost of manufacture is cheaper in this country (R. 39).

The grounds of the decisions below:

Neither the Commission nor the lower courts challenged the credibility of the testimony showing the adequacy of the contractual income yield. There was some criticism by both the Commission and the District Court of the lack of evidence of other instances where entire factory production was wholesaled on a cost plus basis, but such criticism was far from meeting the testimony showing that entire output manufacture on a 6% basis was regarded in the trade as fair and profitable and that the contracts were fair and reasonable.

The Commission, indeed, went to the point of laying down a rule of evidence which would have excluded all evidence possible of production. It said:

"The appellant has failed to produce any evidence which shows actual prices at which Palmolive product was purchased by the Palmolive Company (Delaware) or at which such product could have been purchased in the United States except from the Palmolive Company (Wisconsin). In order to show that the Palmolive Company (Wisconsin) received a fair price for its product it would be necessary to have actual purchases of Palmolive product by the Palmolive Company (Delaware) from unaffiliated manufacturers in the United States and the prices at which such product was purchased from them, but no such purchases existed and, therefore, no such prices were available to enable the Commission to determine the fair value of this product. The test of a fair price is what unaffiliated purchasers will pay for the same product, at the same time, in the same market and in similar quantities" (R. 550).

The result of this was to exclude, not only the best evidence available, but to prescribe a rule which excluded all evidence.

That the Commission closed the door to all evidence of fairness of the contract yield is again manifested by the testimony of its auditor who said in substance that the apportionment formula was adopted on the theory that the statutes *required* its adoption "where the separate accounting method which was used does not, in our opinion, properly reflect the income attributable to Wisconsin" (R. 84).

So the underlying ground of administrative and judicial disregard of the evidence was not lack of credibility or probative weight. The ground rather was that the taxpayer's income could not be measured by the net income from goods sold in Wisconsin and by the usual fair profit derivable from manufacture and wholesale delivery of the remainder of the output of the factory—because such measure failed to include factors of profit which attached to the old business.

That such was the basic ground is indicated early in the Commission opinion, where it is said:

"Granting that corporations do enjoy the fullest freedom in selecting a location for business and that they are subject to no interference in extending business operations, still we do not believe that they may, by sleight-of-hand juggling of Wisconsin earned income or by any mystic wand-waving, cause such income to disappear before our very eyes. We do not believe that drawing the vines over the garden wall to pluck the fruit in any degree lessens the utility of the parent stem" (R. 520).

And again, more concretely, though less poetically, the Commission, after commenting on the intangible value attaching to the trade name, etc. which had been "built up by the successful operation of the business over a long term of years" said:

"It was impossible for the Palmolive Company (Wisconsin) to be stripped of all of the good will of this business when in fact it continued to operate *as an integral part of the combined business.* * * * The good will which attached to the various departments continued to function *for the general success* of the business in the same manner after the reorganization as before, regardless of the fact that the agreement contemplated the ostensible passing of the good will from one arm of this business organization to the other" (R. 533).

Such also appears to have been the basic ground of the decision of the District Court which also did not have before it the decision in the *Rees* case (283 U. S. 183). This is illustrated by the following quotation:

"Though Wisconsin Company attempted to transfer its good will to parent company it necessarily reserved such parts thereof as were involved in the *manufacture* of Palmolive soap under the trademark name according to the trade formulas developed in the past, and in the direct sale of the trademarked article to the trade in Wisconsin" (R. 581).

Again:

"* * * the situation was the same as if the Milwaukee plant and its production *were in fact part and parcel of the parent company.* The creation and use of three corporations could serve no substantial beneficial purpose except to appear to remove income from the state though still creating it within the state" (R. 583).

And again:

"* * * there *appears no reason for the surrender of such profit, which it had demonstrated its ability to earn,* other than to evade the taxes thereon and to appear to convey the same to the parent company for distribution amongst the stockholders without contribution under the revenue laws of Wisconsin" (R. 586) (Italics supplied).

Such also was the basic ground on which the Court of Appeals justified the Commission assessment, holding, in substance, that the product manufactured during the tax years was impressed with a fair share of profit resulting from previously created trade name and good will.

Specification of errors:

The following of those assigned (R. 593) more particularly present the errors here urged:

1. The court erred when it ignored the reorganization which had taken place and assumed the situation was the same after the reorganization as before.

2. The court erred in disregarding separate corporate entities and in considering the various corporations as one corporation.

3. The court erred in sustaining the * * * Commission's action of assessing a tax * * * based on an apportionment of the incomes of several independent corporations which owned no property and transacted no business in Wisconsin.

4. The court erred in failing to hold that the method adopted * * * for determining the taxable income * * * was not authorized by the statutes * * * and was also in violation of the Fourteenth Amendment * * *.

5. The court erred in holding that the tax returns * * * did not correctly set forth the taxable income * * *.

6. The court erred in holding that the inter-company contract * * * was a fraud upon the income tax laws of Wisconsin.

SUMMARY OF ARGUMENT.

I.

The Statement of the Court of Appeals That the Taxpayer Fell "Far Short of its Statutory Duty of Making 'A True and Accurate Statement of its Taxable Wisconsin Income'" Is Without Basis in Statute or Fact.

II.

The Formula Adopted by the Commission Operated To Tax Outside Income.

(a)   The undisputed evidence showed that the income returned by the taxpayer embraced all income fairly derivable from a business of the character and scope of that in fact transacted by the taxpayer in Wisconsin, and, hence, that the Commission formula operated to tax some $3,000,-000 of outside income.

(b)   The Commission assessment is not sustainable on the theory that the product manufactured during the tax years was impressed with a share of income resulting from previously created trade name and good will.   No such income attached to or was realized from the limited business transacted in Wisconsin.   Any such income could be attributable only to business transacted outside the state by the National Company, and was subject to taxation only in a foreign jurisdiction.

(c)   The evidence foreclosed judicial justification of the Commission formula by reconstructing the terms of the inter-company contracts to accord with the judicial view of reasonable terms, and foreclosed the assumption that such reconstruction operated to increase taxable income to an amount as close to the Commission assessment as was determinable from the record.

(d)   Were effect given to the judicial reconstruction of the contract terms a large part of the Commission assessment would be left unaccounted for except as outside income.

III.

In Applying the Statutory Formula, the Commission Acted Without Jurisdiction to the Prejudice of the Taxpayer.

(a) The question of Commission jurisdiction to use such formula, though clearly within the issues, was apparently overlooked by the Courts below.

(b) Wisconsin Statutes exclude jurisdiction to apply the formula in the present case.

ARGUMENT.

I.

The Statement of the Court of Appeals That the Taxpayer Fell "Far Short of its Statutory Duty of Making 'A True and Accurate Statement of its Taxable Wisconsin Income'" Is Without Basis in Statute or Fact.

For the "statutory duty" the Court must have looked to Section 71.09 (3) which provides:

"Every corporation, whether taxable under this chapter or not, shall furnish to the Tax Commission a true and accurate statement on or before March 15th of each year, * * * in such manner and form and setting forth such facts as said Commission shall deem necessary to enforce the provisions of this chapter. * * * Any corporation failing to file any such statement or form shall be subject to a fine. * * *"

Never before was this statute interpreted to mean that a taxpayer makes his return of Wisconsin income under peril of forfeiture of his constitutional rights if Commission or Court should later disagree with him as to what is and what is not income taxable within the state.

The statute has no relation to the enforcement of judicial remedies for an erroneous assessment of tax. That is the subject of a different section (Sec. 71.14), apparently overlooked by the Court, which provides:

"No person against whom an assessment of income tax has been made, shall be allowed in any action or proceeding * * * to question any assessment of income, unless written objections thereto shall first have been presented in good faith to the Tax Commission * * * and full disclosure made under oath of any and all income of such party liable to assessment * * *.''

That the taxpayer made full disclosure was never questioned. Its returns made detailed response to the items of information called for by the blanks (R. 182, 229, 244). Full response was made to the Commission request for further details (R. 192-197). Later the Commission auditor made a so-called field audit (R. 90):

"Mr. VanNatta (the auditor) was given access to all the books and records of all of the companies. He was given every record that he asked for. We gave him our operating statements of all of the companies, balance sheets and everything he asked for" (R. 28).

The auditor testified:

"I found the books of accounts and the records of all of these four corporations that I have referred to accurately kept, as far as bookkeeping accuracy is concerned. They clearly reflected the business transactions of these companies in accordance with the contracts and leases to which I have referred. According to the contracts and agreements I would say that the books have been kept in accordance with them. I found that the tax returns made clearly and accurately reflecting the income in accordance with those contracts and leases, and in accordance with the books" (R. 83, 84, 175, 176).

The comprehensiveness of the Commission audit is indicated by an exhaustive report of over seventy pages, containing upwards of fifty Schedules and Exhibits (R. 308-341).

Following the audit, the taxpayer was notified of the proposed additional assessment, and requested and was allowed a hearing as provided by statute (Sec. 71.12).

At no time during the administrative proceedings, nor in this litigation (until the observation of the Court of Appeals), has there been suggestion or implication of want of fair and full disclosure.

II.

The Formula Adopted by the Commission Operated To Tax Outside Income.

(a) **The Undisputed Evidence Shows That the Income Returned by the Taxpayer Embraced All Income Fairly Derivable From a Business of the Character and Scope of That in Fact Transacted by the Taxpayer in Wisconsin, And, Hence, that the Commission Formula Operated to Tax Some Three Million Dollars of Outside Income.**

This case has been confused and complicated, and much of comment about evading taxes indulged in, through failure to give effect to certain elementary principles.

The income of the taxpayer subject to Wisconsin taxation was only "such income as is derived from business transacted and property located within the state" (Sec. 71.01, 71.02 (3) (d) Wis. Stats.). This excludes jurisdiction to tax outside income, as does the Fourteenth Amendment.

> *Standard Oil Co. vs. Wisconsin Tax Comm.*, 197 Wis. 630, 634; 223 N. W. 85.
>
> *Hans Rees' Sons vs. North Carolina*, 283 U. S. 123.

The location, character, scope and extent of business activities are matters for the determination of the parties, whether corporations or individuals. Wisconsin tax laws do not and constitutionally could not attempt to control their freedom of action. Motive is immaterial. It lawfully may be the express purpose of avoiding taxes.

> *Will of Heymann,* 190 Wis. 97, 104.
>
> *In re Village of Chenequa,* 197 Wis. 163, 169.
>
> *Weeks vs. Sibley* (D. C. N. D. Texas), 269 Fed. 155.
>
> *Fraser vs. Nauts* (D. C. N. D. Ohio), 8 Fed. (2d) 106.
>
> *Iowa Bridge Co. vs. Commissioner* (C. C. A. 8th Cir.), 39 Fed. (2d) 777.

The taxpayer here had no income except that derived from the restricted business transacted in Wisconsin. Its income from Wisconsin sales was admittedly shown by its books and was included in its return. The remainder of its income was solely derived from output manufacture and wholesale to the National Company on a cost plus basis, —a substantially non-risk business of assured return.

Had the cost plus contracts been made at arm's length between strangers, the conclusive measure of the income from the business actually transacted would have been the contract measure.

The contracts having been made between commonly controlled corporations, a different rule applied, but different only in the respect that the contractual *measure* of profit was not conclusive. It became the right and duty of the Commission to scrutinize the measure, but only for the purpose of determining whether it was in fraud of the tax laws and if so to determine what would be a reasonably fair and adequate income yield from the restricted business which the taxpayer was in fact transacting in Wisconsin.

In determining that question the Commission was bound to consider and apply the evidence adduced at the hearing. That it failed to do. In substance it declined even to consider the evidence, or any other evidence within possibility of production. Such arbitrary action alone demanded reversal of its assessment.

> *Northern Pacific vs. Department of Public Works,*
> 268 U. S. 39, 44, 45.

The evidence certainly *tended* to show (as much as did the evidence in the *Rees* case) that the yield derived under the inter-company contracts from the output manufacture and wholesale delivery of the product was fair and reasonable (R. 37, 63, 67); that 6% was the maximum of factory cost (with glycerine deduction) ordinarily derivable under arm's length contracts between strangers; that considering the character and nature of the business such maximum would yield a fair and adequate profit even if entire factory output were manufactured and sold on that basis (R. 62-65, 151, 70, 159, 67, 155); and that the yield from the contracts somewhat exceeded the maximum.

Such evidence was relevant, material and competent. It was of similar character to that erroneously rejected by the commissioner in the *Rees* case, on which this court based its determination that the formula there applied operated to tax producing and marketing income earned in another state.

> *Hans Rees' Sons vs. North Carolina,* 283 U. S.
> 123, 134; 153 S. E. Rep. 850, 854.

It was in substance read out of the case on the erroneous theory, condemned by this court in the *Rees* case and by the Wisconsin court in the *Standard Oil* case (197 Wis. 630), that Wisconsin should be the beneficiary of some unmeasurable additional share of the marketing income which had been enjoyed by the old Company before its owners exercised their legal right to limit the character and scope of the business thereafter to be transacted in Wisconsin.

(b) **The Commission Assessment Is Not Sustainable on the Theory That the Product Manufactured During the Tax Years Was Impressed With a Share of Income Resulting From Previously Created Trade Name and Good Will.**

For such reason, as in substance ruled by the Court of Appeals, "a reasonable profit attributable to this manufacturing function cannot be adequately measured by a percentage of the cost of material and labor and the like." This operated to exclude as immaterial the evidence of the fairness of the contract yield.

It was the view of the court that the above consideration differentiated the *Rees* case. We submit that the contrary is true. It was as much within the legal right of the owner in this case as it was in the *Rees* case to restrict its local operations. As well might it have been claimed in that case as in this that the taxing jurisdiction was entitled to share in the intangible benefit of good will income realized in the marketing state.

The ruling of the court is, we submit, in direct conflict with the decision of the Wisconsin Supreme Court in

Standard Oil Company vs. Wisconsin Tax Commission, 197 Wis. 630, 636; 223 N. W. 85.

"The real basis of defendant's argument seems to be that because the plaintiff company sells a large amount of its products in Wisconsin, its manufacturing profits in other states are increased by reason of the continuity of its operations and increased volume of business resulting from sales made in Wisconsin; and for that reason some of the profits derived from operations carried on without the state are attributable to intrastate operations and so constitute income earned within the state and therefore taxable as Wisconsin income. * * *

"We regard as unsound the argument submitted to sustain the commission's position in this case. If the manufacturing profits of the plaintiff company are increased by means of sales operations in the state of Wisconsin, the converse is true that the sales operations in Wisconsin benefit by the manufacturing operations of the plaintiff corporation in other states. The argument cannot be applied one way and not the other. If it should appear that the manufacturing operations were conducted at a loss in other states, would it be claimed that some part of that loss might properly be charged to sales operations in the state of Wisconsin to diminish the Wisconsin income? We think not."

Standard Oil Co. vs. Wisconsin Tax Comm., 197 Wis. 630, 636-638.

The taxpayer's returned income admittedly included all net income realized from sales to the Wisconsin trade, and consequently reflected all Wisconsin income attributable to past or current advertising or exploitation of the product. The ruling of the court involved the startling assumption that over $3,000,000 of income was attributable to the product manufactured and delivered to the National Company and by it marketed outside Wisconsin. That Company was the only one which contacted with the trade or public, or which could *realize* profit from the trade name or good will. Sales by that Company in outside jurisdictions necessarily embraced the full *realized* income attributable to the product sold. Advertising and exploitation of trade name are of no substantial value except as they create a public demand, and profits from those factors accrue and are realizable only from the marketing activity. Tax laws do not attempt to mortgage future income nor to tax potential or hypothetical income. They reach realized income only, and the taxing power resides alone in the state where realized.

Manifestly tax laws may not say to a resident soap dealer, no matter how valuable his good will or the trade name of his product, or how bright the prospect of future profit, that he shall not go out of the business altogether, or that he shall not confine it to factory production and wholesale to others, or that in case he does so and realizes the income incident to that restricted business he shall be assessed something more on account of hypothetical, unmeasurable and unrealized profit said to be attributable to hangover good will. If he chooses to sell out his marketing business and thus to restrict the character and scope of his activities to output manufacturing on order for an assured margin of profit, thereby eliminating trade name and good will as a factor of realized profit, that is his affair and not the concern of tax laws.

(c) **The Evidence Foreclosed Reconstruction of the Contracts According to the Judicial View of Reasonable Contractual Terms.**

The Court of Appeals enhances cost of manufacturing or factory cost, and hence the base to which is applied the profit percentage, by including therein general and overhead items, such as interest, rental, etc., and also proceeds of glycerine sales, and by assigning glycerine profit to Wisconsin, and by condemning as inadequate the profit percentage. Whereupon the Court concludes:

"We cannot present definite figures specifying the dollars and cents by which the several items discussed would increase the taxpayer's taxable income for these years as returned by the taxpayer. In our judgment the record does not admit of estimates materially better or closer than those which the Tax Commission made in its report and assessments."

Thus to reconstruct the base on which profit percentage is calculated no more justifies the Commission assessment sonal property taxes of $54,126 as were laid on the leased factory equipment (R. 191). The court apparently recognized, though failing to mention, that to whatever extent the taxpayer took deduction for rental paid to Western Operating Company the latter made corresponding return of income (R. 259, 267, 279).

Interest. In ruling that interest paid by the taxpayer should have been included in manufacturing cost, the court treats that item as inferentially very large. The interest paid by the taxpayer during the three years aggregated $64,813 (R. 192, 231, 246), 6% of which amounts to $3,888. In treating the omission of interest from manufacturing cost as so consequential an item, it is possible that the court had in mind the interest of $456,583.29 paid by the Western Operating Company to the National Company during the two years 1925 and 1926 (R. 268, 280),—the payment of which, incidentally, largely accounted for its return of a deficit for those years. That Company made its separate return for each of the three years, taking the interest deduction expressly allowed by Wisconsin statutes, was assessed by the Commission on the basis of such returns, and no additional assessment or reassessment has been made by the Commission against that Company. Its individual income is not involved in this case. It is obvious that the taxpayer here cannot be assessed on account of income of Western Operating Company. But even if we were to assume that the court so far overlooked the fact as to intend the inclusion in manufacturing cost of interest paid by Western Operating Company, as well as that paid by the taxpayer, the resulting increase in taxable income would amount to only $27,395.

than would multiplication of the contractual percentage.

The agreed base was "cost of manufacturing" in the 1924 contract and "factory cost" in the contract for 1925 and 1926. As before noted, the terms were equivalent and had an understood and accepted trade meaning which excluded such items as rent, interest, administrative expense, so-called "middleman's profit" and glycerine proceeds and confined the base to cost of material (less proceeds of glycerine), labor and other costs directly affecting expense of manufacture (R. 63, 66-67).

Indeed, the Commission-furnished tax return blanks assume exclusion of items of that character from "cost of manufacturing" by requiring separate designation of such general costs (R. 230, 231).

As before seen, the testimony was that 6% on factory cost (after glycerine deduction) was the maximum of the profit commonly or reasonably derivable from the manufacture and delivery of private brand soap,—which was the business in question. Substitution of judicial conception as to the items which should make up the base and as to the applicable percentage operates, of course, to read the evidence out of the case.

It is however, appropriate that brief reference be made to the various items of judicial adjustment:

"Middleman's reasonable profit." By this is meant, as we understand the decision, that reasonable profit should have been added to cost to the taxpayer of the raw materials supplied to it by the National Company, thereby enhancing factory cost. The Commission advanced no such claim, nor, so far as we recall, have its auditors or counsel.

The court's view arises out of the fact that the contracts reserved to the National Company the right to purchase and sell to the taxpayer at cost such raw materials as the former should elect (R. 221, 398), and that it supplied to the taxpayer over the three years raw materials to an amount exceeding $25,000,000.

The presumption appears to be indulged that had the National Company and the taxpayer been strangers the latter would have purchased its own materials at a higher price. As matter of fact, the reservation by the National Company of the right to provide the raw materials was for the purpose of maintaining the standard of quality (R. 221, 251). It is of record also that in all the arm's length contracts between the National Company and foreign manufacturers excepting two, the National Company reserved a similar right to purchase and sell at cost, and that in the two (Mexican and Belgian) provisions were inserted having an equivalent result (R. 404, 405, 425, 435, 436, 444, 453, 463, 488, 489, 413, 476). It is of record also that the bulk of all raw materials purchased by the National Company went to the taxpayer (R. 331). Had the latter made the purchases direct, *it would have been its plain duty to have purchased at as low a cost as possible.* With the required volume in excess of $25,000,000 over the three years, it is scarcely conceivable that the taxpayer could not have obtained as low a price as the National Company whose total purchases were but little more.

Rentals. The court refers to the wide variation in the rentals paid to Western Operating Company for the three years: $120,000 for 1924, $234,463 for 1925 and $231,108 for 1926. The rental provided for in the leases was, for the year 1924, $120,000, *plus taxes, insurance and maintenance,* and for the other two years depreciation of plant and equipment plus 5½% of net investment of lessor therein. The court omits to note that for 1924 the taxpayer was assessed real estate taxes of $25,028 *plus* such part of per-

Glycerine sales as taxable income. First should be noted the statement of the court that:

> "The record in respect to glycerine deduction is far from satisfactory. Neither the tax returns made for those years (1925, 1926) nor the corporate books indicate whether or not such deduction from manufacturing cost was *in fact made.*"

It was not unnatural that the returns of the taxpayer should have given the figures for the net cost of "material" (excluding glycerine) rather than the separate figures of gross cost and of glycerine deduction (R. 230).

If, however, the returns left any question as to whether glycerine sales were or were not deducted, the record left no room for question. The testimony explicitly shows that the returns reflected (with minor adjustments not here material) the books of account (Commission Auditor, R. 84), and while the books of account are not in the record, there was explicit testimony that glycerine was not deducted in the accounts for 1924 but was deducted in the ensuing years (R. 49).

The doubt of the court upon the *fact* being thus removed by the record, consideration may be given to its statement that "it would be warrantable to treat all the glycerine sales as taxable income of the Wisconsin Company which created it."

In the first place, thus to treat the proceeds of glycerine sales would be inconsistent with the testimony that 6% of manufacturing cost, after deduction therefor, would represent a fair yield from the business transacted by the taxpayer (R. 37, 63, 67).

It would mean the addition of $1,607,000 (1925—$668,-000, 1926—$939,000) to the $615,567 of income returned by the taxpayer for the same years, making the income for those years nearly four times that actually produced, or sustained by the evidence.

These results fairly show that the court must have proceeded on the erroneous theory before discussed of crediting to Wisconsin unrealized trade name and good will profit (realized and taxable outside Wisconsin) rather than on the theory of assigning to Wisconsin a fair yield from the business which the parties, of lawful right, had determined to transact and were in fact transacting in Wisconsin.

If we were to assume that Wisconsin was entitled to anything on account of crude glycerine sales within its borders *(it was in fact sold and shipped in bulk to glycerine dealers outside the state,* (R. 348) the amount to which it is entitled could in no event exceed the *profit* derived from the sales. *It could not be assumed that the glycerine was produced without cost.* The taxpayer having received the cost of production once, it could not be assumed that he should receive it again plus a profit.

Inasmuch as the glycerine was treated as a by-product, the separate cost of producing it was not reflected in the books. The fair share of cost of production attributable to glycerine may be approximately arrived at, however, and is given in the appended Table IV.

(d) Were Effect Given to the Judicial Reconstruction of the Contract Terms a Large Part of the Commission Assessment Would be Left Unaccounted for Except As Outside Income.

Assuming the inclusion in manufacturing cost of the following judicially inserted items (and the assignment to Wisconsin of profit on sale of glycerine as a factory product), and giving effect to the testimony that 6% of factory cost represents the maximum of profit ordinarily and fairly derivable under arm's length contracts, we get the following income increase for the three year period:

Taxable income as returned and paid	$ 913,787
Increase manufacturing cost by:	
Interest paid by taxpayer	3,889
Rentals paid	45,784
All other administrative and overhead expenses paid	119,179
No credit for glycerine sales	96,469
Total income assuming above additions	$1,179,108
Profit on glycerine sales less profit above included	81,914

Total taxable income on above assumptions $1,261,022 (See Table IV Appendix.)

Thus allowing (contrary to the evidence) for the above judicially referred to additions, we get an aggregate taxable income which is $2,762,805 less than the income resulting from the arbitrary formula applied by the Commission.

No attention is above given to the hypothetical item of so-called "middleman's profit" since that was obviously nonexistent. Nor have we so far disregarded the evidence or tax laws as to assume that glycerine may be treated as a product rather than a by-product for purposes of swelling factory cost but the other way around for purposes of unconscionable additional profit, or that gross sales price constitutes taxable profit or that Wisconsin is entitled to double credit for cost of production. For the above purposes it is enough to assume allowance to Wisconsin (though sale and shipment was interstate) of all glycerine proceeds on any rational assumption realizable as profit.

If now we accept the factory cost base as the parties fixed it ($32,337,439 for the three years (Tax. Comm. Schedule E—2 (line 2, R. 331)) and calculate the percentage thereon required to reach the assessment produced by the Commission formula for the three years, we get 12.44%,—

against the maximum of 6% testified to by the witnesses. If administrative or judicial estimate may thus override undisputed testimony the taxpayer is without protection from arbitrary tax exaction.

Return on Investment:

The Commission made no reassessment of the taxable income returned by Western Operating Company (lessor) and its income is not at issue here. It is involved only as that Company was one of the four companies whose incomes were combined by the Commission (and its Wisconsin property included) for the purpose of determining the income of the *taxpayer* by the apportionment formula. Though the lessor owns the stock of the taxpayer, it is a separate corporate entity, kept separate accounts, made separate returns and is a separate and independent taxable unit under Wisconsin laws.

The Commission auditors sought to justify the Commission's reassessment of the *taxpayer's* income by showing the ratio of returned income of both the taxpayer and the lessor (as adjusted by the Commission) to the combined investment of both (R. 393). Returned income is reduced by large interest deductions which (in case of the lessor, and after depreciation deduction, left to the lessor but about $18,000 of income for 1924 and for 1925 and 1926 left taxable income deficits aggregating near $200,-000). The taxpayer's income as thus adjusted and reduced is then applied to a combined investment within which is reflected obligations to National Company from which accrued the interest deductions. In other words, not only did the auditor combine independent taxable units but in addition he treated the investment as free from the debt and at the same time inconsistently reduced net income by interest paid on the debt.

Proper determination of the ratio of net earnings to the investment which produces them requires of course the disregard of the debt on both sides. When we speak of 7% as a fair return on a public utility property we do not mean 7% after interest on its securities applied to full value without deduction of the debt represented by the securities.

In Table I of the Appendix is shown the return upon the investment of the *taxpayer* yielded by the taxable income returned by the *taxpayer*. The average annual rate of return is 14.38%.

For the purposes of comparison with the erroneous Commission method of combining taxpayer and its lessor (the latter an independent taxable unit whose income is not here at issue) there is appended Table II in which is taken combined Wisconsin investment as given in Commission audit (R. 393) and the returned income of the taxpayer adjusted to the basis of its unencumbered ownership of the factory and equipment leased from Western Operating Company, and thus reflecting net return on combined Wisconsin investment. The resulting average annual return is 8.67%. This from a practically non-risk, assured return business.

For purposes of showing the enormous yield from such a business which would result from the arbitrary Commission formula, Table III is appended. This shows an average annual return on total Wisconsin investment of 27.66%.

III.

The Commission Was Without Jurisdiction to Apply the Statutory Formula.

Federal jurisdiction was vested not alone on denial of due process but on diversity of citizenship. Thus the issue, tendered by the pleadings, of lack of Commission jurisdiction to determine as it did the amount of taxable income of the taxpayer, was clearly before the courts below.

(a) **The Issue Was Apparently Overlooked in the Decisions Below:**

There is no discussion of the statutes in the opinion of the District Court, and they are not referred to in the opinion of the Court of Appeals.

Jurisdiction must be found in the statutes. Jurisdictional statutes may not be extended beyond their express terms.

> *Fisher vs. Standard Oil Co.*, 12 F. (2d) 744 C. C. A. 8th Cir.).
>
> *Fraser vs. Nauts*, 8 F. (2d) 106 (D. C. N. D. Ohio).
>
> *People ex rel. Studebaker Corp. vs. Gilchrist*, 244 N. Y. 114, 115 N. E. 68, 72.
>
> *Pioneer Express Co. vs. Riley* (Cal.), 284 Pac. 663.

An administrative order made without statutory jurisdiction or without or against evidence is an arbitrary act against which courts afford relief.

> *Northern Pacific Co. vs. Department of Public Works*, 268 U. S. 39, 44, 45.

(b) **The Statutes Excluded the Application of the Statutory Formula Adopted by the Commission.**

The material statutes are set out in the Appendix.

Sections 71.01 and 71.02 (3) (d) expressly limit the taxable income to ''such income as is derived from property located or business transacted within the state.''

Section 71.02 (3) (d) expressly provides:

''Persons engaged in business within and without the state shall be taxed only on such income as is derived from business transacted and property located within the state. The amount of such income apportionable to Wisconsin may be determined by an allocation and separate accounting thereof, when, in the judgment of the Tax Commission, that method will reasonably reflect the income properly assignable to this state, but *otherwise* in the following manner: * * *'' (Italics supplied).

Then follows the apportionment formula which the Commission assumed to apply, with provisions authorizing dropping out of one of the three ratios in case it would give an unreasonable final average, and with the added provision that:

"If the income of any such person properly assignable to the State of Wisconsin cannot be ascertained with *reasonable certainty* by either of the foregoing methods, then the same shall be apportioned and allocated under such rules and regulations as the Tax Commission may prescribe" (Italics supplied).

It will be noted that:

1. The apportionment statute is applicable only to a taxpayer who is engaged in business both within and without the state. The taxpayer here, against which the entire reassessment was laid, transacted business *wholly* in Wisconsin. The apportionment formula was entirely inapplicable.

2. The statute expressly contemplates the separate identity of the individual taxpayer, excluding the combination of separate entities. That was disregarded by the Commission. Wholly without authority, it applied the apportionment formula as though the taxpayer and its lessor (the plaintiff) were a single taxpaying unit and made its reassessment against the taxpayer alone.

"The taxing officers of the state are mere administrative agents. They may not devise new forms and methods of taxation, however convenient and useful. They have no more inherent power to tax a corporation upon the income of its stockholders where the stockholder is another corporation than they have where the stockholder is a natural person."

People ex. rel. Studebaker vs. Gilchrist, 244 N. Y. 114, 155 N. E. 68, 72.

3. Even if this were the case of a taxpayer transacting business both within and without the state (which it is *not*), the right to apply the apportionment method is, by the statute, permissible only in the event that "in the judgment of the Tax Commission" (meaning, of course, reasonable and not arbitrary judgment) "determination" of income "by an allocation and separate accounting thereof" will not reasonably reflect the income properly assignable to the state (Sec. 71.02 (3) (d)).

All the business transactions of the taxpayer were shown on its separate books of account. The statute, as well as the Fourteenth Amendment, limited Commission jurisdiction to the assessment of the net income derivable from the limited business in fact transacted. The character and scope of that business was defined in the inter-company contracts, and the results were reflected on the books which the Commission audited. It was easily open to the Commission and it was its duty to ascertain whether the cost plus percentage was a fair measure of profit for the business transacted. Plaintiff showed that it was. The Commission made no effort to obtain further evidence as to the fact, made no request for further evidence, disregarded the *preferred* separate accounting method and without authority applied the apportionment formula.

This contravened the decision of the Wisconsin Supreme Court in

> *Standard Oil Company vs. Wisconsin Tax Commission,* 197 Wis. 630, 638; 223 N. W. 85.

and the decision in

> *People ex rel. Studebaker Corp vs. Gilchrist,* 244 N. Y. 114, 155 N. E. 68, 70.

and was a departure from the method adopted by the Commission itself in

> *Buick Motors Co. vs. Milwaukee,* 48 F. (2d) 801 (C. C. A. 7th Cir.), 43 Fed. (2d) 385 Dist Ct. E. D. Wis.
>
> *Cliff's Chemical Co. vs. Tax Comm.,* 193 Wis. 295.

4. The Commission action was not only in contravention of the statutes above referred to, but also of Section 71.25 (1), which is directed to the very matter of inter-corporate price arrangements, and which expressly authorizes, and impliedly requires, the Commission to:

"* * * determine the amount of the taxable income of such corporation" (not both corporations) "for the calendar or fiscal year, having due regard to the reasonable profits which but for such arrangement or understanding might or could have been obtained from dealing in such products, goods or commodities."

This statute clearly recognizes as lawful inter-corporate price contracts, and thereby carries the plain implication that there shall be no disturbing of the situs or character of the business as actually transacted, and that the Commission function shall be the substitution of such fair yield as would have been obtainable under a similar arm's length contract.

5. Even had the statutes permitted this case to be treated the same as though the National Company alone owned and transacted the business of all the Companies (as the District Court treated it, R. 583), the application of the Commission formula was excluded by Section 71.02 (3) (d), sub-par. 5, which in substance made it the condition of its application to a particular case that it would reflect Wisconsin income with "reasonable certainty."

This was preeminently a case where the formula was bound to reflect a wholly uncertain, arbitrary and excessive measurement of income. The outside marketing business of the National Company was an expanding business to be greatly enlarged by mergers. The Milwaukee factory was producing to practical capacity. The excess supply required and to be required by the National Company was manufactured in an outside factory and other factories in contemplation and since acquired. The scope and extent of the Wisconsin business were substantially constant. Yet the income derived from it, according to apportionment formula, was necessarily up or down, as outside investment, outside cost of manufacturing, and outside sales should be less or more,—factors in no way affecting the character, scope or volume of the business transacted in Wisconsin. Again, the net marketing income of the National Company was vitally affected by the cost of marketing, including not only direct losses, but the millions involved in advertising which was productive or not according to its persistency and effectiveness. Yet, cost of manufacturing in Wisconsin was one of the ratios applied by the Commission (to the great advantage of Wisconsin) and the National Company's cost of sales which, considering advertising cost, might, in any year, pretty much absorb marketing profit, was not included as a ratio factor. Its gross sales might be fairly constant but productive of no substantial profit. Yet under the apportionment formula that would make no difference to Wisconsin.

Indeed, the statute carries on its face confession that each of its three ratios is arbitrary as applied to any business, for it adopts neither but rather the arithmetical average of the three.

In view of the statutes above referred to, Commission adoption of the apportionment formula is understandable only on the theory (condemned both by this Court and the Wisconsin Court) that Wisconsin manufacturing was a factor which helped to produce the outside marketing income,—that such latter income was "Wisconsin fruit * * * of the parent stem" of which that state should have a $3,000,000 share.

Respectfully submitted,

LOUIS QUARLES,
and
HARRY L. BUTLER,
Counsel for Petitioner.

APPENDIX.

The Statutes in Question.

71.01. *Person and subjects taxable.* There shall be assessed, levied, collected and paid a tax on all income received in each calendar year beginning with the year 1920, by every person residing within the state and by every non-resident of the state upon such income as is derived from property located or business transacted within the state, except as hereinafter exempted; provided, that all persons whose fiscal year ends on some other date than December 31, may be assessed on the income of such fiscal year in lieu of the income of the calendar year, at the discretion of the tax commission. This section shall not be construed to prevent or affect the correction of errors or omissions in the assessment of income of former years as authorized by subsection (1) of section 71.10 and section 71.11.

71.02 (3) (d) Persons engaged in business within and without the state shall be taxed only on such income as is derived from business transacted and property located within the state. The amount of such income apportionable to Wisconsin may be determined by an allocation and separate accounting thereof, when, in the judgment of the tax commission, that method will reasonably reflect the income properly assignable to this state, but otherwise in the following manner: There shall first be deducted from the total net income of the taxpayer such part thereof (less related expenses, if any) as follows the situs of the property or the residence of the recipient; provided, that in the case of income which follows the residence of the recipient, the amount of interest and dividends deductible under this provision shall be limited to the total interest and dividends received which are in excess of the total interest paid and allowable as a deduction under section 71.03 (2) during the income year. The remaining net income shall be apportioned to Wisconsin on the basis of the ratio obtained by taking the arithmetical average of the following three ratios:

1. The ratio of the tangible property, real, personal, and mixed, owned and used by the taxpayer in Wisconsin in connection with his trade or business during the income year to the total of such property of the taxpayer owned and used by him in connection with his trade or business

everywhere. Cash on hand or in bank, shares of stock, notes, bonds, accounts receivable, or other evidence of indebtedness, special privileges, franchises, good will, or property the income of which is not taxable or is separately allocated, shall not be considered tangible property nor included in the apportionment.

2. In the case of persons engaged in manufacturing or in any form of collecting, assembling, or processing goods and materials within this state, the ratio of the total cost of manufacturing, collecting, assembling, or processing within this state to the total cost of manufacturing, assembling, or processing everywhere. The term 'cost of manufacturing, collecting, assembling, or processing within this state and everywhere,' as used herein, shall be interpreted in a manner to conform as nearly as may be to the best accounting practice in the trade or business. Unless in the opinion of the tax commission the peculiar circumstances in any case justifies a different treatment, this term shall be generally interpreted to include as elements of cost within this state the following:

a. The total cost of all goods, materials, and supplies used in manufacturing, assembling, or processing within this state regardless of where purchased.

b. The total wages and salaries paid or incurred during the income year in this state in such manufacturing, assembling, or processing activities.

c. The total overhead or manufacturing burden properly assignable according to good accounting practice to such manufacturing, assembling or processing activities within this state.

3. In the case of trading, mercantile, or manufacturing concerns the ratio of the total sales made through or by offices, agencies, or branches located in Wisconsin during the income year to the total net sales made everywhere during said income year.

4. Where, in the case of any person engaged in business within or without the State of Wisconsin and entitled to an apportionment of his income as herein provided, it shall be shown, to the satisfaction of the tax commission, that the use of any one of the three ratios above provided for gives an unreasonable or inequitable final average ratio because of the fact that such person does not employ, to any appreciable extent in his trade or business introducing the income tax, the factors made use of in obtaining such

ratio, this ratio may, with the approval of the tax commission, be omitted in obtaining the final average ratio which is to be applied to the remaining net income.

5. As used in this section the word "sales" shall extend to and include exchange, and the word 'manufacturing' shall extend to and include mining and all processes of fabricating or of curing raw materials. If the income of any such person properly assignable to the state of Wisconsin cannot be ascertained with reasonable certainty by either of the foregoing methods, then the same shall be apportioned and allocated under such rules and regulations as the tax commission may prescribe.

6. Whenever in the opinion of the commission the use of inventories is necessary in order clearly to reflect the income of any person subject to income taxation, inventories shall be taken by such person upon such basis as the commission may prescribe, conforming as nearly as may be to the best accounting practice in the trade or business, and most clearly reflecting the income.

71.09 (3). Every corporation, joint stock company or association, whether taxable under this chapter or not, shall furnish to the tax commission a true and accurate statement, on or before March fifteenth of each year, except that returns for fiscal years ending on some other date than December thirty-first, shall be furnished within sixty days after the last day of such year, in such manner and form and setting forth such facts as said commission shall deem necessary to enforce the provisions of this chapter. Such statement shall be made upon the oath or affirmation of the president, vice-president, or other principal officer and the treasurer of said corporation, joint stock company, or association. All corporations doing business in this state shall also file with the tax commission on or before March fifteenth of each year a schedule of such transfers of its capital stock as have been made by or to residents of this state during the preceding calendar year. Such schedule shall contain the name and address of the seller and the purchaser, date of transfer, and made by or to residents of this state during the preceding calendar year. Such schedule shall be subject to a fine of not less than fifty nor more than five hundred dollars.

71.12. *Notice and hearing.* No additional assessment by office audit or field investigation shall be placed upon the assessment roll without notice in writing to the taxpayer

44

giving him an opportunity to be heard in relation thereto.
Such notice shall be served as a circuit court summons or
by registered mail. Any person feeling aggrieved by such
assessment shall be entitled to a hearing before the tax
commission in the case of corporations or the county board
of review in the case of persons other than corporations,
if within twenty days after receiving notice of such proposed assessment he shall apply for such hearing in writing,
explaining in detail his objections to such assessment. If
no request for such hearing is so made, such assessment
shall be final and conclusive. If a request for hearing is
made the taxpayer shall be heard by the tax commission or
the board of review as the case may be and after such hearing the tax commission or the board of review shall render
its decision regarding such assessment.

71.14. *Exclusive original jurisdiction.* No person
against whom an assessment of income tax has been made
shall be allowed in any action or proceeding either as plaintiff or defendant to question any assessment of income,
unless written objections thereto shall first have been presented in good faith to the tax commission in all cases of
assessment made by such commission or to the county board
of review in case of all assessment made by assessors of
income, and full disclosure made under oath of any and
all income of such party liable to assessment, and unless
such person shall have availed himself of the remedies provided in section 71.12.

71.25 (1). *Corporate tax evasion prevented.* When
any corporation liable to taxation under this act conducts
its business in such a manner as either directly or indirectly
to benefit the members or stockholders thereof or any person interested in such business, by selling its products or
the goods or commodities in which it deals at less than the
fair price which might be obtained therefor, or where a
corporation, a substantial portion of whose capital stock
is owned either directly or indirectly by another corporation, acquires and disposes of the products of the corporation so owning a substantial portion of its stock in such a
manner as to create a loss or improper net income, the commission may determine the amount of taxable income of
such corporation for the calendar or fiscal year, having due
regard to the reasonable profits which but for such arrangement or understanding might or could have been obtained
from dealing in such products, goods or commodities.''

APPENDIX.

TABLE I.

Percentage taxpayer's returned taxable income to taxpayer's investment, including factory and equipment not owned by taxpayer but by its lessor:

1. Returned Income for Year	2. Investment (R. 508, 377-380)	3. Returned Income (R. 182, 230, 245)	4. Percent (of 3. to 2.)
1924	$1,837,831	$298,220	16.22
1925 2,186,128		273,781	12.52
1926 2,329,937		341,786	14.67
Totals 6,353,896		913,787	
Average 2,117,965		304,596	14.38

TABLE II.

Percentage to comparable combined investment of both taxpayer and its lessor, of taxpayer's returned income adjusted to the assumption that it thus owns entire Wisconsin investment, i. e., that it would not receive deduction for rental or interest but would receive deduction for depreciation on factory and equipment of its lessor:

1.	2.	3.	4.	5.	6.	7.
For Year	Combined Wisconsin Investment	Returned Income	Add Rent and Interest Deducted in Taxpayer's Return	Deduct Depreciation per Lessor's Return	Adjusted Returned Income	Per cent (of 6. to 2.)
1924	$4,908,080	$298,220	$120,000	$101,893	$316,326	6.44
1925	4,871,128	273,781	259,837	100,359	433,259	8.89
1926	4,767,977	341,786	270,470	100,224	512,032	10.73
Totals	14,547,185	913,787	650,307	302,476	1,261,617	
Averages	4,849,062	304,596	216,769	100,825	420,539	8.67

Note: (1)

    (a) Taxes on factory and equipment not included in Column 4. because paid by taxpayer as part of rental and deducted in its returns.

    (b) Combined Wisconsin investment (Column 2.) from R. 393, 377-380).

    (c) Returned income (Column 3.) from R. 182, 230, 245.

    (d) Rent and interest as follows: Rent for 1924 ($120,000) from R. 259, for 1925 ($234,463), from R. 267, for 1926 ($231,108) from R. 279; interest for 1924, none, for 1925 ($25,374) from R. 236, for 1926 ($39,361) from R. 246.

(2) Net obligations of taxpayer and of its lessor (Western Operating Company) to National Company are represented in combined Wisconsin investment, Column 2. above. Therefore, in determining ratio of return upon investment, net earnings should not be diminished by payments of interest on such obligations, as appears to have been done in Commission Exhibit F. R. 393.

TABLE III.

Percentage Commission reassessed income to combined investment of both taxpayer and its lessor:

1.	2.	3.	4.
Reassessed Income for Year	Combined Wisconsin Investment	Commission Reassessment	Per cent (of 3. to 2.)
1924	$4,908,080	$1,297,968	26.44
1925	4,871,128	1,357,979	27.87
1926	4,767,977	1,367,880	28.68
Totals ...	14,547,185	4,023,827	
Average ..	4,849,062	1,341,275	27.66

Note: (1) Investment (Column 2) from R. 393, 377-380.

(2) Reassessed income (Column 3) from R. 320.

TABLE IV.

Effect on Taxable Income of Certain Items Referred to by Court.

	1. Net Taxable Income Returned and Taxed	2. 6% on all Interest Paid by Taxpayer	3. 6% on all Rent Paid	4. 6% on all other General Expense	5. 6% on Proceeds Glycerine (R. 348)	6. Total Col. 1 to 5	7. Glycerine Profit Over Proportionate Share of Cost. (Note)	8. Total Col. 6 and 7	9. Income Assessed by Comm. (R. 320)	10. Excess Col. 9 over Col. 8
1924 (R. 258-264)	$298,220	$ 2	$11,248	$39,408	$.....	$348,878		$348,878	$1,297,968	$949,090
1925 (R. 229-241)	273,781	1,525	17,709	36,224	40,083	369,322	$33,978	403,300	1,357,979	954,679
1926 (R. 244-255)	341,786	2,362	16,827	43,547	56,386	460,908	47,936	508,844	1,367,880	859,036
Totals..........	913,787	3,889	45,784	119,179	96,469	1,179,108	81,914	1,261,022	4,023,827	2,762,805

Note: Profit on Glycerine (Col. 7 above) estimated as follows:

	1. Total Gross Sales (including proceeds glycerine) (R. 230, 245, 348)	2. Proceeds Glycerine (R. 348)	3. Per Cent Glycerine to Total Sales (of Col. 2 to Col. 1)	4. Total Manufacturing Cost Including Glycerine (R. 230, 245, 348)	5. Glycerine Share of Manufacturing Cost Col. 3 x Col. 4)	6. Profit on Glycerine (Col. 2— Col. 5)	7. Less 6% Col. 6 (already included Col. 5 above table)	8. Net Profit Glycerine (Col. 6— Col. 7) Carried to Col. 7 above table
1925	$12,856,560	$668,049	5.118	$11,687,781	$598,181	$69,868	$35,891	$33,978
1926	12,805,999	939,765	7.338	11,465,627	841,348	98,417	50,481	47,936

MAY 31 1932

CHARLES ELMORE CROPLEY
CLERK

IN THE

Supreme Court of the United States

OCTOBER TERM, 1931

No.  62

THE PALMOLIVE COMPANY, a Delaware corporation,
Petitioner and Appellant below,

vs.

W. J. CONWAY, CHARLES D. ROSA, EDWARD L.
KELLEY, as members of the Wisconsin Tax Commission, and PATRICK McMANUS, as Treasurer of Milwaukee County,

Respondents and Appellees below.

RESPONDENTS' BRIEF

JOHN W. REYNOLDS,
Attorney General of Wisconsin,
THEO. W. BRAZEAU,
Special Counsel for
Wisconsin Tax Commission,
LEO J. FEDERER,
Counsel for Respondents.

INDEX

I

II

IV

V

VI

v

AUTHORITIES CITED

IN THE

Supreme Court of the United States

OCTOBER TERM, 1931

No.

THE PALMOLIVE COMPANY, a Delaware corporation,
Petitioner and Appellant below,

vs.

W. J. CONWAY, CHARLES D. ROSA, EDWARD L.
KELLEY, as members of the Wisconsin Tax Commission, and PATRICK McMANUS, as Treasurer of Milwaukee County,

Respondents and Appellees below.

RESPONDENTS' BRIEF

PRELIMINARY STATEMENT

This is a suit in equity brought by the appellant as successor to the Palmolive Company of Wisconsin to enjoin the collection of income taxes assessed and determined by the Wisconsin Tax Commission for the years 1924, 1925 and 1926. These taxes were assessed by the Wisconsin Tax Commission under the provisions of Chapter 71, Wisconsin Statutes for 1925, and Chapter 71, Wisconsin Statutes for 1927, known as the Income Tax Law.

Judgment was entered in the District Court for the Western District of Wisconsin, Judge Lindley presiding, dismissing the complaint, except as to the tax against the Buckingham Agency.

The case was fully heard and argued in the District Court and a very able opinion rendered thereon by Judge Lindley.

Palmolive Company vs. Conway, et al., 43 F. (2) 226.

In that opinion Judge Lindley very clearly analyzes all of the questions raised here by petitioner and very ably and fairly deals with those questions. The decision of Judge Lindley is fully sustained on appeal to the Court of Appeals for the Seventh Circuit in the decision written by Judge Alschuler.

Palmolive Company vs. Conway, et al., 56 Fed. (2) 83.

The statement of facts in petitioner's brief is substantially correct but is mixed throughout with statements of conclusions and insinuations which need not be mentioned at this time.

Reference to the record where it is claimed to be conceded that the income of petitioner was accurately reported shows that the concession was that it was accurately reported assuming that the contracts were to govern the income. (R. 83, 84) In referring to the contract between the parent company designated by petitioner as the National Company, and the Wisconsin Company, counsel for petitioner refers to these contracts as contracts for the *manufacture* of soap. In truth and in fact the contracts were for the *sale* to the National Company of all soap manufactured by the Wisconsin Company and not merely a *manufacture* of soap for the National Company. (R. 219, 395)

SUMMARY OF ARGUMENT

I

The Wisconsin Tax Commission, Judge Lindley nor the Circuit Court of Appeals did not decide this case on the ground that the corporate domicile and situs of business activities of petitioner could not be determined by the corporation itself.

Decision of Tax Commission (R. 515).
Palmolive Company vs. Conway, et al., 43 F. (2) 226–232. (District Court)
Palmolive Company vs. Conway, et al., 56 F. (2) 83. (C. C. A.)

The decision in this case does not depend at all on such conclusion.

II

The decision of the Tax Commission, the decision of Judge Lindley nor the decision of the Circuit Court of Appeals was based upon the proposition that income taxes could be levied upon business transacted and property located without the state of Wisconsin.

Decision of Tax Commission (R. 515).
Palmolive Company vs. Conway, et al., 43 F. (2) 226.
Decision of Judge Lindley (R. 577).

III

The contracts in question were arbitrary and did not reflect the true income of the Wisconsin Company. There is adequate evidence in the record to show that these contracts were not binding upon the state of Wisconsin in so far as the income of the Wisconsin Company was concerned.

Section 71.25, Wisconsin Statutes of 1927. (Appendix Pet. Brief p. 44)

Section 71.25, Wisconsin Statutes of 1925. (Appendix Pet. Brief p. 44)

Buick Motor Co. vs. Wisconsin Tax Commission, 43 F. (2nd) 385.

Buick Motor Co. vs. City of Milwaukee, 48 F. (2nd) 801 (C. C. A.) 284 U. S. 655 (Writ denied).

Palmolive Company vs. Conway, et al., 43 F. (2nd) 226.

People ex rel. Studebaker Corp. vs. Gilchrist 244 N. Y. 114.

Proctor & Gamble vs. Sherman, 2 F. (2nd) 165.·

Cliffs Chemical Co. vs. Wisconsin Tax Commission, 193 Wis. 295, 277 U. S. 574.

Judson Freight Forwarding Co. vs. Commonwealth 242 Mass. 47, 136 N. E. 375.

Rensselaer vs. Irwin, 239 F. 739.

Rensselaer vs. Irwin, 249 F. 726.

West & Strong Ry. vs. Malley, 246 F. 675.

Houston Belt Ry. vs. United States, 250 F. 1.

Shaffer vs. Carter, 252 U. S. 37, 64 L. Ed. 445.

Underwood Typewriter Co. vs. Chamberlain, 254 U. S. 113, 65 L. Ed. 165.

Wabash Ry. Company vs. American Refrigerator Transit Co., 7 F. (2nd) 335.

Hans Rees' Sons vs. North Carolina, 283 U. S. 123.

Bass, Ratcliff & Gretton Co. vs. State Tax Commission, 266 U. S. 271.

National Leather Co. vs. Massachusetts, 277 U. S. 413.

IV

The Tax Commission was not bound to accept the conclusion of petitioner's witnesses but was free to analyze such testimony and consider the surrounding facts and circumstances including the admissions of such witnesses on cross-examination.

V

The Tax Commission the trial judge and the Court of Appeals fully understood and analyzed the issue and the decision of both the Commission and the learned trial judge were based upon the record and upon a proper analysis of the issues.

VI

The Commission the learned trial judge and Court of Appeals properly construed and applied the Wisconsin statutes. There was no denial of equal protection of the laws and due process as guaranteed by the fourteenth amendment to the constitution of the United States.

> *Underwood Typewriter Co. vs. Chamberlain*, 254 U. S. 113.
>
> *Cliffs Chemical Co. vs. Tax Commission*, 193 Wis. 295, 277 U. S. 574.
>
> *Judson Freight Forwarding Co. vs. Commonwealth*, 242 Mass. 47, 136 N. E. 375.
>
> *Bass, Ratcliff & Gretton vs. State Tax Commission*, 266 U. S. 271.
>
> *Michigan Law Review*, Vol. 29, page 600.
>
> *Harvard Law Review*, Vol. 44, page 935.
>
> *National Leather Co. vs. Commonwealth of Massachusetts*, 277 U. S. 413.
>
> *Hans Rees' Sons vs. North Carolina*, 283 U. S. 123.

The last mentioned case, so often mentioned in appellant's brief, fully sustains the contention of appellee.

ARGUMENT

I

THE WISCONSIN TAX COMMISSION JUDGE LIND-
LEY NOR THE CIRCUIT COURT OF APPEALS
DID NOT DECIDE THIS CASE ON THE GROUND
THAT THE CORPORATE DOMICILE AND SITUS
OF BUSINESS ACTIVITY COULD NOT BE DE-
TERMINED BY THE CORPORATION

Petitioner contends that the state may not constitutionally interfere with the right of directors and stockholders
of a corporation to determine corporate domicile and situs
of business activities as well as the character and extent of
the business to be transacted in any state. We are confi-
dent the court will not be misled by any such straw man set
up by the petitioner. We do not contest this general proposition of law asserted by counsel and which is amply sustained by authority but insist that it is not a question in
this case. The Tax Commission freely conceded the right
of the petitioner to change its place of residence and the
situs of its corporation or to do any other thing it desired
for the purpose of its legitimate corporate business. We
concede that the corporation could change its situs even
though this was done for the purpose of avoiding Wisconsin taxes, but the distinction must always be borne in mind
between *avoiding* tax liability and *evading* tax liability.
The Wisconsin Tax Commission says in its opinion:

> "The Commission cannot question the right of cor-
> porations to remove property and business from this
> state and incorporate in foreign states but the mere
> incorporation in another state does not ipso facto re-
> move the situs of a business. Of course, the Commis-
> sion does not subscribe to the foolish doctrine that once
> a Wisconsin corporation, always a Wisconsin corpora-

tion and once a Wisconsin taxpayer, always a Wisconsin taxpayer, and we are in accord with the taxpayer's self-evident statements as to the unrestricted rights of a corporation to move its business as it pleases without regard to geographical boundaries and to transfer its assets, discontinue its Wisconsin business, market its products and perform other functions, all as declared in taxpayer's brief. The exercise of any such rights is not to be hampered in any degree by their effects upon the net profit taxable in Wisconsin.'' (R. 519–20)

This shows that the Wisconsin Tax Commission fully conceded petitioner's general proposition, but if business, notwithstanding the complicated efforts of petitioner, still remained in Wisconsin, it was still subject to taxation in Wisconsin. Counsel contends that by taxing the Palmolive Company of Wisconsin on the income which the Commission contends was actually earned by that company in Wisconsin, the Commission is ignoring this principle of law. We are then back to the original question involved in this case.

The learned trial judge also conceded petitioner's undisputed proposition of law but correctly concluded that it was not involved in this litigation. The learned trial judge says:

"The Commission contends that it ignored no constitutional rights of plaintiff but recognized all of such rights and rendered its decision in accordance therewith. The question as presented is whether with the same business in Wisconsin as before, the corporation has by its contracts so manipulated its organization and contracts and relations to cover up the true income attributable to Wisconsin property and business; whether the court may go behind the contracts of correlated corporations or whether it is bound by the same. If the contracts are binding upon the state, if no part of the alleged additional income is attributable to the state of Wisconsin, no relief can be had, but if the circumstances are such that it follows that the contracts were made for the express purpose of evading taxation, that is, to attempt to remove, *without in fact removing,* income earned in the state of Wisconsin to a place beyond the state, then the court has a right to go beyond the contract and ascertain the facts."

  Palmolive Company vs. Conway, et al., 43 F. (2nd) 226 at 228.

There was never any question anywhere involving the trite proposition stated by petitioner. The question involved was as to whether or not the company did remove the taxable income in question from Wisconsin to Illinois or some other place. It is conceded that the same manufacturing plant remained in Wisconsin after the contracts and that its sales were somewhat larger (R. 333) and that the price was about the same (R. 501) and the cost of manufacturing the same and if anything reduced. (R. 501) The question considered and decided by the Tax Commission and Judge Lindley and the Court of Appeals was not the right of the company to remove from the state but as to whether the National Company owning all of the stock of the Western Operating Company, which owned all the stock of the Wisconsin Company, with the same officers and directors, could by an intercompany contract arbitrarily by such contracts alone remove the taxable income of the Wisconsin Company from the state.

II

THE DECISION OF THE TAX COMMISSION THE DECISION OF JUDGE LINDLEY NOR THE DECISION OF THE COURT OF APPEALS WAS BASED UPON THE PROPOSITION THAT INCOME TAXES COULD BE LEVIED UPON BUSINESS TRANSACTED AND PROPERLY LOCATED WITHOUT THE STATE OF WISCONSIN

The decision of the Tax Commission is based upon the proposition that the income tax was derived from the business transacted and property located within the state. The decision of Judge Lindley and the Court of Appeals was also based upon the same proposition.

A reading of the Tax Commission's decision clearly shows that the Commission earnestly and intelligently sought to determine the true income of the Wisconsin corporation earned in Wisconsin. It proceeded under the laws of Wisconsin governing this subject, which material statutes are as follows:

Section 71.01 of the Wisconsin Statutes for 1925 provides:

> "There shall be assessed, levied, collected and paid a tax on all income received in each calendar year beginning with the year 1920, by every person residing within the state and by every nonresident of the state upon such income as is derived from property located or business transacted within the state, except as hereinafter exempted; * * *"

There is no exemption material to the inquiries in this case.

This section remained the same in 1927 except that it provided for an average net income.

Section 71.02 (3) (c) of the Wisconsin Statutes for 1925 provides:

"Income from mercantile or manufacturing business, rentals, royalties or the operation of any farm, mine or quarry, or from the sale of real or personal property for the purposes of taxation shall follow the situs of the property or business from which derived, * * *"

This section is the same in the laws of 1927.

Section 71.25, Laws of 1925, entitled Corporate Tax Evasion Prevented, provides:

"When any corporation liable to taxation under this act conducts its business in such a manner as either directly or indirectly to benefit the members or stockholders thereof or any person interested in such business, by selling its products or the goods or commodities in which it deals at less than the fair price which might be obtained therefor, or where a corporation, a substantial portion of whose capital stock is owned either directly or indirectly by another corporation, acquires and disposes of the products of the corporation so owning a substantial portion of its stock in such a manner as to create a loss or improper net income, *the commission may determine the amount of taxable income of such corporation for the calendar or fiscal year,* having due regard to the reasonable profits which but for such arrangement or understanding might or could have been obtained from dealing in such products, goods or commodities."

In 1927 an additional paragraph was added as follows:

"(2) For the purpose of this chapter, whenever a corporation which is required to file an income tax return, is affiliated with or related to any other corporation through stock ownership by the same interests or as parent or subsidiary corporations, or whose income *is regulated through contract* or other arrangement, the tax commission may require such consolidated statements as in its opinion are necessary in order to determine the taxable income received by any one of the affiliated or related corporations.''

The tax in question was levied under these provisions of the statutes. There was no attempt to tax income earned beyond the state borders and no contention is made that the Tax Commission could constitutionally so do. In considering the income of the affiliated corporations, the Tax Commission did so only for the purpose of determining the income earned in Wisconsin as it had a lawful right to do. This Court has approved an apportionment under the same circumstances.

> *Underwood Typewriter Co. vs. Chamberlain*, 254 U. S. 113.
> *Hans Rees' Sons Co. vs. North Carolina*, 283 U. S. 123.
> *Bass, Ratcliff & Gretton Co. vs. State Tax Commission*, 266 U. S. 271.
> *National Leather Co. vs. Mass.*, 277 U. S. 413.
> *Cliffs Chemical Co. vs. Tax Commission*, 193 Wis. 295, 214 N. W. 447, 277 U. S. 574.
> *Judson Freight Forwarding Co. vs. Commonwealth*, 242 Mass. 47, 136 N. E. 375.

Section 71.25 of the Wisconsin statutes is constitutional and the Tax Commission had the right to administer the same.

> *Cliffs Chemical Co. vs. Tax Commission*, 193 Wis. 295, 214 N. W. 447, 277 U. S. 574.

This Court refused to review the Cliffs Chemical Company case, thus holding such statute constitutional.

> *Cliffs Chemical Co. vs. Tax Commission*, 277 U. S. 574.

12

Proctor & Gamble Distributing Co. vs. Sherman, 2 F. (2nd) 165.
People ex rel. Studebaker Corp. vs. Gilchrist, 244 N. Y. 114.

It is freely conceded that where the business transacted in the state may be determined with certainty by a separate accounting, the Commission has no right to consider any other method. The income of the Standard Oil Company in Wisconsin could be so determined and it was rightly held that the Commission had no right to consider any other method of arriving at the income in that case.

Standard Oil Co. vs. Wisconsin Tax Commission, 197 Wis. 630.

This case was not disregarded or miscontinued by the Court of Appeals.

In determining the tax in the case at bar, it was necessary for the Commission to proceed under the authority or in the manner provided in section 71.25 of the statutes.

In passing this statute the legislature recognized that corporate organizations furnished a very ready means of evading state income taxes and hence it gave the Commission the right, when a substantial portion of the stock of one company is owned by another and the local company conducts its business in such a manner as to either directly or indirectly benefit the members or stockholders thereof by selling its products or goods in which it deals at less than fair price which might be obtained therefor, to inquire into and determine the reasonable profit which but for such arrangement or understanding might or could have been obtained from dealing in such products, goods or commodities. Under this section the Commission rightly inquired into the fairness of the inter-company contracts entered into between the Palmolive National Company and the Wisconsin Company in view of the complete domination of the Wisconsin Company by the National Company and the full ownership of all stock of the Western Operating Company by the National Company and the full ownership of all stock of the Wisconsin Company by the Western Operating Company. (The Western Operating Company is now the Palmolive Company, the plaintiff in this action.) Petitioner's argument then gets back to the question as to whether the contracts were fair and reasonable, and if so, whether the Wisconsin Tax Commission rightly determined the earnings of the Wisconsin Company in Wisconsin.

The case at bar is the same as the Buick case recently decided by Judge Geiger and affirmed by the Court of Appeals and which this Court refused to review. The only difference is a difference of degree. The Buick Company was bolder in its greed to transfer the earnings of its Wisconsin branch outside of the state.

> *Buick Motor Co. vs. Wisconsin Tax Commission*, 43
>   F. (2d) 385.
> *Buick Motor Co. vs. City of Milwaukee*, 48 F. (2nd)
>   801, 284 U. S. 655.

The case at bar is in no way similar to the Studebaker and Proctor & Gamble cases in which there was a clear attempt to assess income earned outside of the state, but the court in those cases fully recognized and endorsed the right which the Wisconsin Tax Commission exercised in this case.

> *Proctor & Gamble Distributing Co. vs. Sherman, id.*
> *People vs. Studebaker Corp., id.*

III

THE CONTRACTS IN QUESTION WERE ARBI-
TRARY AND DID NOT REFLECT THE TRUE IN-
COME OF THE WISCONSIN COMPANY. THERE
IS ADEQUATE EVIDENCE IN THE RECORD TO
SHOW THAT THESE CONTRACTS WERE NOT
BINDING UPON THE STATE OF WISCONSIN IN-
SOFAR AS THE INCOME OF THE WISCONSIN
COMPANY WAS CONCERNED

Petitioner contends that the taxpayer accurately reported all income actually received by it and promptly paid
the state income tax computed thereon. The record dis-
closes, however, that it reported only the income *as reflected by the contracts* in question and paid the state income tax only as computed thereon. (R. 83–84) It is there
stated in the testimony:

"I found that the tax returns made clearly and accurately reflecting the income *in accordance with those
contracts* and leases and in accordance with the books."

Under this head it is contended that there is affirmative
and undisputed proof in the record by fair and impartial
testimony, that the contracts fully reflected the Wisconsin
income and all of the income which would have resulted if
the contracts had been made at arm's length and between
strangers. It is the contention of petitioner that such testimony establishes the fairness of the contracts in question
as a verity in this case and that the Commission had no
right to take into consideration any other fact except the
testimony of petitioner's witnesses and conclusions stated
by them; that the Commission had no right to consider all
of the surrounding circumstances and relations of the in-
ter-allied corporations in determining the question of the

fairness of these contracts and no right to analyze such testimony.

It is the contention of respondents that such testimony does not establish without dispute that the contracts in question are reasonable and fair. The Tax Commission and the Trial Court and Court of Appeals gave every consideration to such testimony and discussed the same at length in their opinions. We respectfully invite the court's attention to the careful analysis of this testimony given in the opinion of the Tax Commission. (R. 542–552) Judge Lindley also gave these contracts the most careful consideration and stated the contention of petitioner as follows:

> "Plaintiff insists that the factory cost plus percentage contract was a fair and equitable one; that other manufacturers in America manufacture soap upon similar basis; that it contracts for the manufacture of soap in foreign countries upon substantially the same basis; that such a contract between two such distinct entities as two corporations *must be accepted at its face value;* and that to ignore or go behind such contracts is to interfere with the constitutional rights of the parties to contract."

And then Judge Lindley adds:

> "This contention might be of persuasive force were the facts in the record of such seeming innocent import."

> "But it must be observed in this connection that other soap manufacturers who manufacture soap upon a cost plus basis do so only to the extent of a small part of their capacity."

Petitioner asserts that its testimony as to the fairness of these contracts is undisputed and must be accepted as conclusive.

It becomes necessary, therefore, to analyze this testimony.

1. It is stated in petitioner's brief that the National Company contracted similarly with unaffiliated companies for the manufacture of Palmolive soap for its foreign business.

We submit that the evidence does not show that such contracts are on the same footing with the contracts in question.

a. They involve the purchase of soap in foreign countries where conditions differ greatly from conditions in the United States. (R. 118) Foreign countries do not have the improved machinery and efficient organization of American companies and hence according to the testimony of Mr. Lansing of the petitioning company, (R. 39) the cost of manufacture in foreign countries is larger than the cost in America. Hence, a cost plus basis on the same percentage is much more advantageous in the case of foreign countries.

b. The foreign contracts do not involve the entire output of any manufacturer. Mr. Lansing also testified that as a matter of fact they purchase but a small portion of the total production of these plants in foreign countries. (R. 40 and 119)

c. Only one of these contracts (France) involves a cost plus percentage provision. (R. 443–452 at 445–446, 497) Every one of the others is based on fixed allowances for profit. (Argentina, R. 403–412, price R. 405; Belgium R. 413–422, price R. 414; Cuba R. 422–434, price 427; Denmark R. 434–443, price R. 436; Germany R. 452–462, price 454; Italy R. 462–475, price R. 469; Mexico R. 475–487, price 478; Sweden R. 487–496, price 489)

d. The analysis and comparison of these foreign contracts one with the other shows that the terms of these contracts differ from each other and from the terms of the contracts between the Palmolive Company of Wisconsin and the Palmolive Company of Delaware. (R. 497) The factory cost per gross for Palmolive soap in 1926 was $3.52 in the case of the French manufacture and $6.59 in the case of the Mexican manufacture. (R. 120, 497) The sale price of the Palmolive Company of Wisconsin to the Palmolive Company of Delaware under the contracts in question was $3.48 in 1926 and this sale price was six per cent above factory cost. It follows that the factory cost of Palmolive soap of the Wisconsin Company was $3.28 per gross in 1926. In 1927 the factory cost in France was $4.34, in Germany $4.08, in Holland $4.46, in Italy $4.72 and in Mexico $5.49. (R. 120) On the basis of the Mexican cost in 1926, the profit per gross to the Mexican manufacturer on a cost plus six per cent basis would be nearly forty cents while to the Wisconsin Company it would be less than twenty-one cents, giving the Mexican company about one hundred per cent advantage. The sum and substance of the foreign contracts show clearly the unfairness of the Wisconsin contract.

On the basis of the French contract, which is the lowest price and which is the only cost plus contract in the whole list of foreign contracts, the price to the Wisconsin Company on the same basis should have been cost plus twelve per cent instead of six per cent. The price paid to foreign companies ranged from $3.69 to $6.97 per gross in 1926, while the price paid to the Wisconsin Company was only $3.48. In addition to this, the Wisconsin Company was required under its contracts, to ship the goods directly to the purchasers and stand all losses on lost or returned shipments. (R. 398, paragraph 9; R. 221, paragraph 7) In addition thereto, the Wisconsin Company was required to pay a share of the national advertising. (1924 contract R. 222, paragraph 9; 1925 contract R. 399, paragraph 11) Evidently the Wisconsin Company had to make all collections as the contract provides that the Delaware company only guarantees to collect accounts for goods sold to chain stores. (R. 221, paragraph 8; R. 398, paragraph 10) The Wisconsin Company is responsible under the contracts for deliveries and collections. (See contracts.)

> 2. Petitioner contends that the National Company manufactured soap for others on a comparable cost plus basis.

The soaps referred to were the private brands. (R. 37) They are manufactured for such companies as Woolworth, Atlantic & Pacific Tea Company, Owl Drug Company, Gimbel Brothers and others who buy upon a close percentage and where the competition is keen, as appellant admits. (Brief, p. 45) In fact, the competition is so keen that they not only manufacture at cost plus one to six per cent. but as testified by Mr. Lansing of the plaintiff company, *"in fact in some cases at a loss. The company has always done that."* (R. 37) Surely this class of business which is sold so closely that in some cases they even sell at a loss, cannot be made a basis for proving the fairness of the contract of one branch of the Palmolive Company with another branch where no such competition exists and where the whole production is sold.

> 3. Appellant contends that these contracts are shown conclusively to be fair and reasonable because other large soap companies customarily made soap on a cost plus basis ranging in factory cost from one to six per cent.

As stated by Judge Lindley with reference to this testimony:

> "But it must be observed in this connection that other soap manufacturers who manufacture soap upon a cost plus basis do so only to the extent of a small part of their capacity. Having manufacturing busi-

nesses of their own, producing their own products, but not thereby exhausting their entire productive capacities, they make use of their additional capacities by working on cost plus contracts for others as fillers or as supplementary productions which furnish some profit from sources that otherwise would be entirely idle. There is in the record an eloquent silence as to any manufacturer who has built or bought a factory for the purpose of devoting it entirely to cost plus production. There is an equally eloquent silence as to any manufacturer employing all the productive capacity of his plant to such small profit contracts.''

Palmolive Co. vs. Conway, et al., 43 F. (2nd) 230.

The witness Wrisley testified that he sold private brand soaps on a basis of cost plus six per cent or less. (R. 62) He further testified that only forty to fifty per cent of their business was on a cost plus basis and cost plus ran from one to six per cent. He does not testify that if his company sold its *entire output* at cost plus six per cent or even three per cent, it would be a prosperous business even though the company had no other customers. This was not from a knowledge of his own business at all and he did not testify that his company could do this. (R. 65)

S. C. Jones of the Kirk Company also testified and his testimony is relied upon as being conclusive upon the subject. He testified:

"As a matter of fact, we have for years been manufacturing all the way from six per cent and even one per cent and *sometimes below cost* on certain occasions.'' (R. 66)

Surely he was not testifying to contracts made in the ordinary course of business as companies could not afford to contract to manufacture for less than cost. He further testifies as follows:

"Approximately ten per cent of the total volume of our business is conducted on cost plus contracts." (R. 70)

Also:

"I stated that in some cases we contracted for the sale of soap below cost. We have done that at times to help take care of the overhead." (R. 70)

He also testified that his profits would not be as great if he was disposing of his entire production under these kind of contracts. (R. 70) Very evidently they constituted a small part of his business and he was dealing with private brands (R. 67) and was taking these contracts to fill out and keep down overhead. It is true this witness testifies in a general way that it would be profitable that if the Kirk Company's business was conducted on a cost plus basis similar to the Wisconsin Company's contract, it would be a profitable enterprise, but he also testifies that the profits would not be as large if his entire production was sold under these kinds of contracts. (R. 70) This same witness testified that the cost of manufacture of the Kirk-olive soap, which is comparable to the Palmolive, by his company would run *from $5.50 to $6.00* almost twice the price paid under the contracts *in total*. (R. 153) The undisputed evidence shows that the cost to manufacture the Palmolive soap in 1924 was $3.34, in 1925 $3.45 plus, and in 1926 $3.28 plus. (R. 501)

These figures are arrived at by deducting the percentage in addition to cost which was paid to the Wisconsin Company by the National Company under its contract. Under a three per cent contract, the Kirk Company would receive $5.67 taking the minimum cost of $5.50, and $6.36 taking the maximum cost of $6.00, as testified to by Mr. Jones. In other words, the Kirk Company would be getting $2.33 per gross higher than the contracts between the National

Company and the Wisconsin Company. In 1924 the difference would be still more exaggerated when the cost plus 3% contract was in force. In 1924 the Kirk Company would get $2.91 more per gross than the Wisconsin Company got from the parent company, in 1925 $2.70 more and in 1926 $2.88 more.

It is this testimony of the fairness of the Wisconsin contract which petitioner wants the Tax Commission to swallow whole without any analysis whatsoever. The petitioner asks the Tax Commission to take the testimony of Mr. Jones and Mr. Wrisley that they consider these contracts fair without any comparison of cost, relationship of the companies or any other factor. It is extremely significant that if companies are anxious to get contracts such as the one in question, that the Palmolive Company has never entered into such a contract with any other soap company in the United States nor did the Palmolive Company in Wisconsin ever manufacture for any one else on any such basis. Mr. Lansing, the only officer of the Palmolive Company who testified for that company, says:

> "In our experience we have never made contracts with American manufacturers on a cost plus basis. We have never had occasion to do that. The only cost plus contract in the United States which we have is that existing between the Delaware corporation, the Palmolive Company of Delaware as it existed between 1924 to 1926, inclusive, and with the Palmolive Company of Wisconsin." (R. 40)

Of course, the Palmolive Company of Wisconsin, which was a mere creature and dominated by the Palmolive Company of Delaware, with the same officers, had no opportunity to make any contract with any one else.

The Wisconsin Tax Commission was entitled to determine the income of the Wisconsin Company on what it could reasonably make as an income from its business and not what it had left after making the contracts in question even though the contracts did leave it some profit. The contracts are not necessarily fair or reasonable even though they left a profit if they took away the reasonable profit which the company might have earned selling its products at a fair price.

IV

THE COMMISSION DID NOT DISREGARD THE EVIDENCE PRODUCED BY THE PETITIONER WITH REFERENCE TO THESE CONTRACTS

The Commission fully analyzed the testimony produced by petitioner with reference to the fairness of the contracts in question. The Commission found from the analysis of foreign contracts that they were not in point and that only one of said contracts was on a cost plus basis and that such contracts showed affirmatively that the Wisconsin contract was unfair and unjust. This testimony has been analyzed under the previous head.

The testimony of American soap manufacturers shows that they only took a very small percentage of business on a cost plus percentage basis and that considering the cost of these companies on a cost plus percentage basis, they would receive many times the profit which the Palmolive Company of Wisconsin received under the contracts in question. The testimony further showed that the Palmolive Company never entered into contracts with any other company in the United States on the terms contained in the contracts with its Wisconsin Company. Nor did the Wisconsin Company enter into any such contract with any other company at any time. The Commission further analyzed said contract in view of the relationship of all of the companies and the profit the Wisconsin Company had made in prior years with the same plant manufacturing the same soap and with the same or a larger capacity.

The analysis of these contracts and the relationship of the parties shows that the contracts were made without any reference to business and economic factors so as to arbitrarily determine the amount of income to be reported for taxation in Wisconsin and so as to take from Wisconsin the taxable income earned by the Wisconsin Company and to shift such income outside of the state.

The circumstances and facts surrounding these contracts are as follows:

A. The relationship of the companies show that the two companies were not dealing at arm's length and that the contracts were an arbitrary arrangement.

(1) The Palmolive Company (Delaware) owned all of the stock of the Western Operating Company.

(2) The Western Operating Company owned all of the stock of the Palmolive Company (Wisconsin).

(3) The officers and directors of all companies are practically identical. (R. 502–5, 525)

(4) The plant, machinery and equipment used by the Palmolive Company (Wisconsin) was owned entirely by the Western Operating Company.

(5) The entire output of the Palmolive Company (Wisconsin) is *subject* to purchase by the Palmolive Company (Delaware) even to the extent that the Palmolive Company (Wisconsin) could be deprived of product necessary for its trade in Wisconsin.

(6) The Palmolive Company (Delaware) has control of the entire production of the Palmolive Company (Wisconsin) and sells this product everywhere except to the trade in Wisconsin.)

B. The terms of the 1924 operating contract between the Palmolive Company (Wisconsin) and Palmolive Company (Delaware) were at great variance with the terms of the 1925 operating contract.

(1) Under these contracts the Palmolive Company (Wisconsin) sold its product to the Palmolive Company (Delaware) at cost plus 3% in 1924; and at cost plus 6% in 1925 and 1926.

(2) The 1924 contract made no provision for payment of interest to the Palmolive Company (Delaware) while the 1925 contract provided for the payment of 5½% interest to the Palmolive Company (Delaware) on the intercompany balance.

C. The terms of the 1924 lease of the Western Operating Company plant, machinery and equipment to the Palmolive Company (Wisconsin) were at great variance with the terms of the 1925 lease.

(1) The 1924 lease provided for a rental charge of $120,000.00 per year against the Palmolive Company (Wisconsin).

(2) The 1925 lease provided for a rental which consisted of 5½% of the book value of the plant plus the annual depreciation.

D. The terms of these contracts were not interpreted in the same manner in 1924 as they were in 1925 and 1926.

(1) These contracts made *no mention* of the treatment of glycerine sales as they might relate to cost but in 1924 glycerine sales were *not deducted* from factory cost, while in 1925 and 1926 they were *deducted* from factory cost before the cost plus percentage was applied.

The glycerine sales of the Wisconsin Company in 1924 were $493,842.23. The price of glycerine was going up and the sales in 1925 were $663,049.46 and in 1926 were $939,765.05. On substantially the same quantity of glycerine produced in 1925 and 1926 as in 1924, the sales of glycerine amounted to one and one-half as much in 1925 and nearly double in 1926. (R. 348) It therefore appeared to the plaintiff that the Wisconsin income under the terms of its written contract would be greatly increased if the sales of glycerine were not taken care of. Therefore, without any provision in the contract, the glycerine sales were deducted in 1925 and 1926 from the factory cost before figuring the 6% profit on manufacturing. The plaintiff seeks to explain the omission to take into account the item of nearly $500,000.00 for glycerine sales for 1924 by stating that it was overlooked in the rush of business of reorganizing the company and making the various contracts and arrangements in question, and yet no provision was made in the 1925 or 1926 contract for glycerine sales, and if an error was discovered it was never corrected on the books, the witness for the company stating that it was too much ''clerical work.'' (R. 130)

With the ability of the Palmolive organization, it would seem, that a small item of $500,000.00 would not be so easily overlooked and when found would be speedily accounted for.

(2) That is, in 1924 the 3% was applied to the total factory cost of main product and by-product whereas in 1925 and 1926 the 6% was applied to factory cost after first deducting glycerine sales.

(3) The glycerine sales were sufficiently large in amount so that factory cost of main product and by-product plus 3% was larger than factory cost *less* glycerine sales plus the larger percentage of 6%.

Example:

1924	$10,000,000 + ($10,000,000 × 3%) =	$10,300,000
1925 & 26	$10,000,000 — $500,000 + [($10,000,000 — $500,000) × 6%] =	10,070,000
	Difference	$230,000

Petitioner seeks to justify changing the situation with reference to glycerine on the ground that the universal custom is to regard glycerine as a by-product and deduct the sales of glycerine from the cost of manufacture. It is significant that the price of glycerine so advanced that while the sales in 1924 were only $493,000 in 1925 they had gone up to $668,000 and in 1926 to $939,000, while the percentage paid added to cost in 1924 and 1925 had gone up from three per cent to six per cent. The 1924 contract makes no mention whatsoever of glycerine, but in 1924 the company claims to have discovered the error in failing to deduct the sales of glycerine from the cost. (R. 130) In 1925 a new contract was made between the National Company and the Wisconsin Company . This contract specifically deals with the factors which are to be reckoned as costs and also factors which are not to be reckoned as costs. Nowhere does the contract define that glycerine is to be deducted from the cost as a factor. (R. 395 at 396)

Custom only controls a contract where the contract is silent on the question. When the terms are fixed by the contract, parties cannot claim a custom as a part of the contract.

> *Francis H. Liggett & Co. vs. West Salem Canning Co.,* 155 Wis. 462.
> *Saner vs. Stein,* 174 Wis. 185, at 199.

Had glycerine not been deducted from the cost of manufacture in 1925 and 1926, the income of the Wisconsin Company would have included the sales of glycerine as a part of its income and also six per cent on the glycerine sold as additional income. The additional income to Wisconsin wuld have been nearly $1,000,000. A tax on this additional sum would be about $70,000 for the year 1926 alone, about $36,000 for 1924 and about $50,000 for 1925—in all an additional tax of approximately $155,000.

(4) The 1924 operating contract between the Palmolive Company (Wisconsin) and the Palmolive Company (Delaware) made no provision for the payment of interest to the Palmolive Company (Delaware) on intercompany balances. For that year no interest was charged by the Palmolive Company (Delaware) on the intercompany balance. (R. 219)

(5) There appears to be no written contract between the Palmolive Company (Delaware) and the Western Operating Company which provided for the payment of interest to the Palmolive Company (Delaware) on the intercompany balance. In 1924 the Palmolive Company (Delaware) did not charge the Western Operating Company with interest on the intercompany balance, but' in 1925 and 1926 interest was charged at the rate of 5½% per annum.

E. The Western Operating Company realized a net loss in 1925 and 1926 on the rental of property to the Palmolive Company of Wisconsin.

(1) The following figures illustrate this point:

	1925 (R. 267–9)	1926 (R. 279–80)
Rent received	$234,463.22	$231,108.62
Less depreciation	*100,359.03**	*100,224.13**
	134,104.19	130,884.49
Less interest on intercompany balance	*223,716.99**	*232,866.30**
Net Loss from Rental	*$89,612.80**	*$101,981.81**

* Italics denotes Red.

(2) That is, the Western Operating Company was charged more interest by the Palmolive Company (Delaware) on intercompany balances than the net rent received from the Palmolive Company (Wisconsin) so that if these interest charges were proper, there was in fact no rental

income reported by the Western Operating Company to Wisconsin on these properties during 1925 and 1926.

(3) The situation with respect to 1924 was almost as bad because only an $18,106.52 net rental was shown by the Western Operating Company for that year on a $3,000,000 plant.

(4) The smaller the rental paid by the Palmolive Company (Wisconsin) to the Western Operating Company, the smaller the cost of the product of the Palmolive Company (Wisconsin) upon which the cost plus percentage was applied and therefore the smaller the Palmolive Company (Wisconsin) profit on goods sold to the Palmolive Company (Delaware).

F. The 3% and 6% on factory cost which was paid to the Palmolive Company (Wisconsin) under the operating contracts of 1924 and 1925, respectively, did not represent the net profit realized by the Palmolive Company (Wisconsin) on sales to the Palmolive Company (Delaware).

(1) The contract provides that the cost plus percentage be applied to factory cost, which did not include all expenses. (R. 219, 395)

(2) The 1925 operating contract even mentioned certain expenses which could not be included as factory cost. (General overhead expenses such as interest, management and the like.) (R. 396)

(3) The *net* profit percentage, therefore, was much smaller than 3% in 1924 or 6% in 1925 and 1926.

(4) The Wisconsin Company was to stand losses on shipments and make collections. (R. 219, 395)

(5) The Wisconsin Company was obligated to pay a proportion of advertising. (Contracts, R. 219, 395)

G. The consolidated book capital and surplus of the Palmolive Company (Wisconsin) and the Western Operating Company was reduced to a mere nominal figure through the reorganization.

(1) The capital and surplus just before the reorganization was $10,486,395.01 for the Palmolive Company (Wisconsin) and the consolidated book capital and surplus of the Palmolive Company (Wisconsin) and the Western Operating Company combined immediately after the reorganization was $22,420.84. (R. 377)

COMPUTATION

Capital and Surplus just before reorganization (Net assets)	$10,486,395.01
Net assets to Palmolive Company (Delaware) in reorganization	4,808,014.04
Net assets remaining for Palmolive Company (Wisconsin) and Western Operating Company	$5,678,380.97
Intercompany account balances due the Palmolive Company (Delaware) by the other two companies as a result of the reorganization	5,655,960.13
Consolidated book capital and surplus of the Palmolive Company (Wisconsin) and Western Operating Company immediately after reorganization........	$22,420.84

(2) This $22,420.84 of consolidated capital and surplus was supposed to represent a net investment of $5,678,380.97 in Wisconsin land, buildings, machinery, equipment and inventories of the Western Operating Company and the Palmolive Company (Wisconsin).

(3) The reduction in capital and surplus to the nominal figure of $22,420.84 was accomplished by the creation of intercompany balances payable to the Palmolive Company (Delaware) in the amount of $5,655,960.13.

(4) The $22,420.84 consolidated book capital and surplus plus the open account balances of $5,655,960.13 in fact

represents the true investment of the Palmolive Company (Wisconsin) and the Western Operating Company.

(5) The petitioner has erroneously used the nominal capital and surplus in an attempt to justify the small earnings reported by the Palmolive Company (Wisconsin) and the Western Operating Company for taxation in Wisconsin.

H. The stockholders of the Palmolive Company (Wisconsin) received large amounts of dividends prior to the reorganization but the holding company (Palmolive Company, Delaware) did not receive any dividends from 1924 to 1926, inclusive, from its Wisconsin subsidiaries. (R. 164–5)

(1) The dividends paid to the stockholders of the Palmolive Company (Wisconsin) for the three years prior to the reorganization were as follows:

	Cash Dividends	Stock Dividends	Total	
1921	$394,731.64	0	$394,731.64	(R. 564)
1922	538,411.56	$495,289.34	1,033,700.90	(R. 567)
1923	706,598.37	3,748,045.06	4,454,643.43	(R. 570)
Total ..	$1,639,741.57	$4,243,334.40	$5,883,075.97	

(2) The Palmolive Company (Delaware) did not receive any dividends, as such, from its Wisconsin subsidiaries during 1924 to 1926, inclusive. However, dividends in fact were received by the Palmolive Company (Delaware) through the operation of the cost plus contracts and in the form of interest on created intercompany balances.

I. The Palmolive Company (Delaware) regarded the Wisconsin business as a branch of the group for all purposes excepting state income taxes.

(1) Mr. Lansing, assistant secretary, in his testimony indicated how the office at Milwaukee was regarded. He

referred to the *"branch* accounting work at Milwaukee.*"* (R. 24)

(2) For federal income tax purposes the Palmolive Company (Wisconsin), the Western Operating Company and Buckingham Agency were consolidated with the Palmolive Company (Delaware). (R. 171–2)

(3) No portion of the federal income taxes of the group were charged against the Palmolive Company (Wisconsin) or Western Operating Company. (R. 171–2)

(4) The Palmolive Company (Wisconsin) shipped direct to customers of the Palmolive Company (Delaware) outside the state just as though they were one and the same company. The loss or miscarriage of shipments was treated as expense of the Palmolive Company (Wisconsin) as though the Palmolive Company (Wisconsin) was dealing direct with the customers as a branch of the group. (R. 219–395)

(5) The Palmolive Company (Delaware) apparently collects the accounts receivable of the Palmolive Company (Wisconsin) which arise out of sales to chain stores in Wisconsin. (R. 219–395)

(6) The Palmolive Company (Delaware) advertised for the Palmolive Company (Wisconsin). (R. 219–395)

(7) The contract provides that the Palmolive Company (Delaware) may supply its needs first and may control the amount of product which the Palmolive Company (Wisconsin) may sell to the trade. (R. 219–395)

(8) The intercompany accounts were in fact branch house accounts. The only difference is that a nominal profit was left on the books of the Wisconsin companies whereas in branch accounting all of the profits are transferred to the home office through the branch house account.

(9) The record also indicates that the Western Operating Company had no employees or office except a mailing

address and that the books were kept for it by the other two corporations. (R. 143)

(10) All of this shows that the Western Operating Company, while it was a separate legal entity, was not regarded as such for any purposes except for the Wisconsin income tax.

(11) For the year 1927 the Palmolive Company (Wisconsin) and the Western Operating Company filed a consolidated Wisconsin income tax return although no request was ever made to the Tax Commission for permission to file in this manner. (R. 288–303) While it is true that these corporations were merged on December 12, 1927, their status for the greater part of 1927 was identical with their status during 1924, 1925 and 1926 insofar as their general relation to each other was concerned. It is rather inconsistent for the company to regard these two companies as a unit for income tax purposes during the entire year 1927 and at the same time contend that the same companies should be considered separately for state income tax purposes during 1924, 1925 and 1926. The voluntary consolidation of these two companies for income tax purposes for the period in 1927 prior to their merger is an unconscious admission on the part of the group that at least two companies should be considered together for Wisconsin income tax purposes; and the intercompany relations and activities between the Palmolive Company (Delaware) and these two corporations were closer and even more interwoven than between the Palmolive Company (Wisconsin) and the Western Operating Company.

J. The various companies in this group operated as one and were indifferent as to the method of treating important items on their books and the income reported to Wisconsin would have been still lower and even more ridiculous if such items had been charged against the Wisconsin business.

(1) Although a glycerine item of about $500,000.00 was said to be incorrectly handled on the books in 1924, no adjustment was ever made for such item. (R. 130)

(2) Although the intercompany balance due the Palmolive Company (Delaware) from the Palmolive Company (Wisconsin) existed during 1924, no charge was made against the Palmolive Company (Wisconsin) for interest for that year. (R. 132–3)

(3) Although the intercompany balance due the Palmolive Company (Delaware) from the Western Operating Company existed during 1924, no charge was made against the Western Operating Company for that year, whereas charges were made for interest for 1925 and 1926 without any written agreement to that effect. (R. 132)

(4) In 1925 the Palmolive Company (Delaware) made a written agreement with the Palmolive Company (Wisconsin) requiring the latter to pay interest on its intercompany balance but no written contract was made requiring the Western Operating Company to pay interest to the Palmolive Company (Delaware) on its intercompany balance. (R. 219–395) (R. 132)

(5) The Palmolive Company (Delaware) paid all of the federal income taxes for the group based upon a consolidated income tax return of the group, but none of these federal taxes were charged to the Palmolive Company (Wisconsin) or the Western Operating Company and none were paid by these two companies. (R. 172)

K. The contracts between the Palmolive Company (Wisconsin) and the Palmolive Company (Delaware) assumed that the Palmolive Company (Wisconsin) transferred all of its good will to the Palmolive Company (Delaware) in the reorganization whereas the entire good will was not in fact transferred.

(1) The good will continued to function for the general success of the various departments of the business as a

whole in the same manner after the reorganization as before.

(2) The good will could not be separated from the assets of this business as a whole, because these assets were all used to maintain and increase the same good will that existed at the time of the reorganization.

(3) The accounting authorities agree that the good will cannot be separated from the assets which assist in the creation, maintenance and growth of the good will of the business. Dr. Yang's "Good Will and Other Intangibles" devotes an entire volume to this subject.

It is true that the good will, trade marks, trade names, etc., were transferred to the National Company in form. The good will of this business, however, was built up beginning with the B. J. Johnson Company from 1894 to 1923 at its plant in the City of Milwaukee. The good will which is claimed to subtract so much from the Wisconsin company's earnings was carried by the Wisconsin Company at no stated value and after the transfer was set up on the books of the National Company at $1.00. The Wisconsin Company, after such transfer of intangibles to the National Company, continued to operate its plant in Milwaukee the same as it had always been operated, manufacturing practically the same amount of soap under the same conditions. This soap, as petitioner concedes, was not made under any secret process or under any magic recipe. It is the contention of the Tax Commission that a paper transfer of such good will could not take from the Wisconsin corporation anything of value. The Commission in its decision says:

"The assets transferred to the Palmolive Company (Delaware) were taken over at book value and no value was assigned to the good will which the appellant contends was taken over by the Palmolive Company (Delaware). Although this good will was built up over a long period of years by the successful operation of the entire business, including all of the departments of the Palmolive Company (Wisconsin), the agreement contemplated turning over this entire good will to the newly created parent company, the Palmolive Company (Delaware) in such a manner as to part with it for one purpose and still retain it for another purpose.

"It was impossible for the Palmolive Company (Wisconsin) to be stripped of all the good will of this business when in fact it continued to operate as an integral part of the combined business."   (R. 532–3)

Good will is *not* something that can be transferred and separated from an established business or segregated from one part of the business and attached to another.

"Good will is the result of the employment of capital in some established business. It augments its value and is an incident to the conduct of the enterprise. It exists at the place where the business is carried on, and gives value to the enterprise because of the benefits that are likely to come to a successor and which arise from being connected with its reputation."
Lindemann vs. Rusk, 125 Wis. 210 at 233.

"Why indulge in a technical difference, which, from a broad standpoint is a mere play on words? In a broad sense, good will is, after all, the value which attends and characterizes a business as a going industry and has developed and become attached thereto in the course of time."
Appleton Water Works Co. vs. Railroad Commission, 154 Wis. 121 at 155.

"The good will of the relator aside from that purchased of Mr. Johnson, is the result of exercising its corporate franchises and carrying on its business in this state *and is inseparable from that business.* It is the product of an investment of capital in this state and the exercise here of the privilege for which the tax was laid. To hold that it was not capital employed in this state, upon the ground that the domicile of the corporation is in West Virginia, where it never transacted any business nor earned any good will by fair dealing and efficient method, would exalt form above substance. As the good will is the result of the employment of capital and an incident to an established business, it can exist for no practical purpose in the state where the relator was organized and where it never invested any capital nor did any business. The good will of the relator belongs to its old and well-established business which is conducted wholly in this state. It is as much a part of the business as the books which it publishes. * * * The mere fact that good will is intangible does not take it out of the state, so far as the right of taxation is concerned, because it is inseparably attached to property which is tangible, located in this state."

People ex rel A. J. Johnson Co. vs. Roberts, 159 N. Y. 70, 45 L. R. A. 126, at 130.

Dr. Yang states on page 5 of "Good Will and Other Intangibles" as follows:

"Receivables are usually paid at maturity. Securities possess considerable marketability. On the other hand, good will and government grants of various sorts, while valuable in a sense, cannot be disposed of or converted into cash without disorganizing the entire business to which they are so closely attached."

Also on page 14 and 15:

"Since good will, for example, becomes a valuable property only when it comes to be of such an unusual character as to give rise to an advantage over a normal competitor, it is a thing that does not belong to the general market, but is confined to the particular business in which it exists."

It is apparent that the transfer of good will to the National Company detracted nothing from the earning power of the Wisconsin corporation. According to counsel's argument, the trade marks, good will and sales constitute the great important part of this business. In the case of Buick Motors Company and Burroughs Adding Machine Company, both of which cases were decided by Judge Geiger in the Eastern District of Wisconsin, the emphasis was placed wholly upon the importance of the manufacturing end of the business by the plaintiff. It seems to depend entirely upon which end of the business is in Wisconsin. The Commission, however, fully recognized the importance of sales, good will and every other factor of the business in making its apportionment of the income properly assignable to the state of Wisconsin. The manipulation of the various allied companies was largely a matter of pen and ink.

(4) Wisconsin was charged with national advertising that helped to create and maintain good will but according to petitioner's contentions the Palmolive Company (Wisconsin) could have no good will. (R. 219–395)

L. The price received by the Palmolive Company (Wisconsin) from the Palmolive Company (Delaware) for its product is entirely out of proportion to the price paid by the trade for the same product; and the gross profit allowed to the Palmolive Company (Wisconsin) by the Palmolive Company (Delaware) by the contracts is entirely out of proportion to the gross profit earned by the group on such product. (R. 501)

1.

	Average price per Gross received by the Palmolive Co. (Wis.) from Palmolive Co. (Dela.) (R. 501)	Average price per Gross received by the Palmolive Co. (Wis.) from the trade in Wisconsin (R. 501)	Average price per Gross received by the Palmolive Co. (Dela.) from the Trade (R. 501)
1924	$3.44	$9.20	$9.26
1925	3.66	9.14	8.98
1926	3.48	9.38	9.18

2.

	Average gross profit per gross realized by Palmolive Co. (Wis.) on sales to Palmolive Co. (Dela.)	Average gross profit per gross realized by Palmolive Co. (Wis.) on sales to trade in Wisconsin	Average gross profit per gross realized by Palmolive Co. (Dela.) on sales to the trade
1924	10¢	$5.86	$5.82
1925	21¢	5.59	5.32
1926	20¢	5.90	5.70

3.

	Sales per Tax Return Palmolive Co. (Wisconsin) (R. 564–567)	Cost of Sales Palmolive Co. (Wisconsin) (R. 570–583)	Gross Profit Reported Palmolive Co. (Wisconsin) (R. 230–245)	
1921	$16,060,659.93	$ 7,946,337.19	$ 8,114,319.74	
1922	20,125,279.24	8,874,209.15	11,251,070.09	
1923	22,372,654.28	10,781,324.06	11,591,330.22	
1924	11,081,181.67	10,000,809.77	1,080,371.90*)	Under
1925	12,188,510.98	11,350,118.35	838,392.63*)	Con-
1926	11,866,233.96	10,975,549.37	890,684.59*)	tract

*Includes gross profit on Palmolive Company (Wisconsin) sales direct to trade in Wisconsin.

No change in manufacturing costs, change in production, change in output or change in sales or price, justifies this tremendous change in Wisconsin income which these contracts produced or attempted to produce.

V

THE TAX COMMISSION THE LEARNED TRIAL JUDGE NOR THE COURT OF APPEALS MISCONCEIVED THE ISSUE

Petitioner contends that the opinions of the Tax Commission and Judge Lindley and Court of Appeals merely involve challenge of the conceded legal right to determine the situs and scope of its business activities. We invite a careful reading of the opinion of the Tax Commission and also of the learned opinion of Judge Lindley and the Court of Appeals and submit that such reading will show a clear conception of the issues involved, to-wit: *As to whether a parent company can contract away the income of one of its subsidiaries without in any degree removing the business and income of the subsidiary from the state where earned.* The Tax Commission Judge Lindley and Court of Appeals considered the issue as to whether such attempted contracts were in fact fair and reasonable and went behind the corporate entities under a right supported by numerous decisions, to determine the real character of the relationship and the *real earnings* of the subsidiary.

It is not true, as petitioner assumes, that the Tax Commission after the reorganization of these companies in 1923, continued to attribute to Wisconsin the same earnings as had always been attributed to that state. In truth and in fact, it reduced the average percentage of earnings in Wisconsin from 89.027% prior to 1924, to an average of 55.276% after that date or a reduction of 33.751%. (R. 317, 328). Judge Lindley in commenting on this evidence, says:

> "The Tax Commission did not allocate to Wisconsin all of the profit upon the goods manufactured in Wisconsin. Whereas in 1921, 1922 and 1923 substantially ninety per cent of the profits were found to have accrued in Wisconsin, in the years 1924, 1925 and 1926 the apportionment to Wisconsin was only 55.28%. The increased apportionment of 33% to the territory outside of Chicago was found to be due to the removal of activities other than manufacture out of the state."
>
> *Palmolive Company vs. Conway, et al.,* 43 F. (2nd) 231.

In the same decision Judge Lindley says:

> "In other words, the Tax Commission found that the Wisconsin Company and plaintiff had, through entirely

legal means, removed from the state annual income of $1,321,000.00 or six times as much as had previously been earned without the state, and that though the total profits from manufacture and sale had increased, the total income earned within the state was only about two-thirds what it had been. It reduced earned Wisconsin income to two-thirds of its former amount and increased the income out of the state six times."

The following table is the Commission's computation of Palmolive net income and shows the decided increase in income ascribed to outside business and property after the reorganization:

BEFORE REORGANIZATION

	Total Income (R. 312)	Wisconsin Income (R. 322)	Outside Income
1921	$1,355,098.77	$1,221,784.15	$133,314.62
1922	3,548,505.08	3,171,050.59	377,454.49
1923	1,156,940.84	1,019,407.12	137,533.72

AFTER REORGANIZATION

	(R. 322)	(R. 322)	
1924	$2,385,870.50	$1,297,967.80	$1,087,902.70*
1925	2,748,958.57	1,357,978.74	1,390,979.83*
1926	2,852,168.06	1,367,879.96	1,484,288.10*

* These amounts include net income on activities which had been outside the state before the reorganization and also the net income from activities transferred at the time of the reorganization.

It will be noted that the outside income of the Wisconsin Company was found by the Tax Commission to be in 1924 over $1,000,000.00 as against $137,000.00 in 1923. In fact, the outside income after the reorganization was eight times as much as before.

In other words, it appears without question that the Tax Commission recognized fully the right of petitioner to remove its activities out of the state and dropped out of the taxation such part as the Commission found was so removed.

VI

THE WISCONSIN TAX COMMISSION NOR THE COURT OF APPEALS DID NOT MISCONSTRUE NOR MISAPPLY THE WISCONSIN STATUTES SO AS TO DENY TO THE PETITIONER THE EQUAL PROTECTION AND DUE PROCESS GUARANTEED BY THE FOURTEENTH AMENDMENT

The question presented to the Tax Commission was to determine the true taxable income of the petitioner earned in Wisconsin. This was not reflected in the books and accounts of this company. The income reflected in the books was the income under the fictitious inter-company contracts. No evidence was offered by the petitioner to show what part of its business was done outside of the state of Wisconsin and no evidence was offered by petitioner apportioning the amount earned in Wisconsin and the amount earned elsewhere by the group of companies constituting the unit known as the Palmolive Company. These companies were inseparably connected. The Palmolive Company of Wisconsin conducting the manufacturing plant in the city of Milwaukee had a gross profit in 1923 of over $11,000,000.00. With the same equipment, the same business and a slightly excessive product, the gross reported profit in 1924 was slightly over $1,000,000.00, in 1925 slightly over $800,000.00, and in 1926 about $900,000.00. (R. 564, 567, 570, 183, 230 and 235) By means of these contracts, petitioner contends that the earnings of this company so disappeared and were no longer taxable in Wisconsin. The earnings of the Wisconsin Company were attempted to be transferred by these contracts outside of the state to the parent company or to the Western Operating Company. As Judge Lindley well stated:

"The plaintiff and the Wisconsin Company were not charitable institutions. The Wisconsin Company was not in the manufacturing business purely for altruistic purposes, but was created and operated for pecuniary profit and there appears no reason for the surrender of such profit which it had demonstrated its ability to earn, other than to evade the taxes thereon and to appear to convey the same to the parent company for distribution amongst the stockholders without contribution under the revenue laws of Wisconsin."

Palmolive Company vs. Conway, et al., Id.

The case at bar is not analogous in any manner to the case of *Standard Oil Company vs. Wisconsin Tax Commission,* 197 Wis. 630 which the petitioner claims the Court failed to properly apply. In that case there were no contracts attempting to contract away the Wisconsin income. The income of the Wisconsin business was clearly reflected on the books of the Wisconsin branch, and hence there was no necessity of going beyond the accounts kept in Wisconsin. The case at bar is different. Here there is no income reflected on the books of the Wisconsin Company except under the contracts. It was necessary for the Commission to go to the books of all of the different corporations in order to ascertain the true amount which should be allocated to the state of Wisconsin. On this subject, the Commission says:

"When the combined activities of a business are so closely related and interdependent upon each other as in this case, it is impossible by the use of arbitrary contracts and arrangements to segregate income and determine just what income is attributable to any one corporation or to the manufacturing or selling activity.

Any scheme of assigning taxable income under such conditions, which results in a high rate of return on investment for one corporation or for one department of the business, and a low rate of return for another corporation or for another department, is arbitrary, and unreasonable. If the business was actually losing money and these arbitrary contracts had assigned a fictitious taxable income to Wisconsin, the Tax Commission could not and would not tax such income.'' (R. 539)

Suppose under the conditions existing in this case the contract should have been so framed as to give to the Wisconsin corporation only a nominal profit from all of its manufacturing operations of $25.00 per year, would the plaintiff contend that the Tax Commission was helpless to make any apportionment of income in order to determine the true profits on the Wisconsin business? Certainly the Tax Commission had a right, if the contracts are so framed as to fail to reflect the income of Wisconsin business, to adopt a rule which in its judgment equitably apportioned to the Wisconsin Company its true return on its property and business. The Wisconsin statute, section 71.02 (3) (d) provides a rule of apportionment in cases of companies or persons transacting business within and without the state. Subdivision 5 of the same section provides that if the income of any such person properly assignable to the state of Wisconsin cannot be ascertained with reasonable certainty by the methods of apportionment set forth, "then the same shall be apportioned and allocated under such rules and regulations as the Tax Commission may prescribe.'' While the statute is not expressly made applicable to a situation exactly as the one at issue, yet the Tax Commission being obliged to use some method of apportionment, was justified in using the method approved by the legislature as a just basis for such apportionment and applying it to the situation at hand. There is nothing in the statute, as petitioner concedes, which requires the Commission to close its eyes to a situation such as presented to it in this case.

It is not true, as stated by petitioner, that the Commission is attempting to deny its right to transfer its property outside of the state or organize separate corporations as it sees fit, nor is it true that the Commission has attempted to tax income derived from business outside of the state of Wisconsin. In fact, the Commission expressly and affirmatively recognized the change in the situation of the plaintiff company after 1923 and recognized that a large part of its income was taken outside of the state and gave effect fully to such situation. This appears from the decision of the Commission which we quote as follows: (R. 520-21)

"In this case the actual removal of a portion of the physical properties and the sales and administrative offices from the state had a material effect upon the income theretofore properly taxable within Wisconsin, and no attempt has been made to tax the income so removed. This is shown by the fact that a smaller apportionment percentage was used by the Tax Commission in determining the corrected taxable income for the period following the reorganization. The average of the apportionment percentage for Wisconsin used by the Commission for the years 1921 to 1923, inclusive, immediately preceding the reorganization, was approximately 89%, while for the years 1924 to 1926, inclusive, immediately following the reorganization, the average apportionment percentage was approximately 55%. This substantial reduction of approximately 34% in the apportionment percentage for Wisconsin was brought about almost entirely by the actual removal of sales and administrative activities from the state at the time of the reorganization and from the increased inventories carried at branches located outside the state following the reorganization.

"In addition to the reduction in taxable income occasioned by the substantial decrease in the apportionment percentage for Wisconsin, all non-apportionable income following the residence of the recipient, such as dividends and interest, was removed from the state. None of the interest and dividends received by the Palmolive Company (Delaware) for the years 1924 to 1926, inclusive, was taxed in Wisconsin, while for years prior to 1924, all income of this nature was fully taxable.

"The following schedule shows what income is recognized by the Tax Commission as having been properly removed from the state by the actual removal of property and business at the time of the reorganization:

APPORTIONMENT PERCENTAGES USED BY TAX
COMMISSION

1921		90.162%)	
1922		89.363%) ......Average 89.027%	
1923	(R. 521)	87.555%)	
1924		57.860%)	
1925		55.403%) ......Average 55.276%	
1926	(R. 521)	52.565%)	

Reduction 33.751%

Apportionment per cent for 1923 (the year before reorganization) (R. 521)   87.555%

Apportionment per cent for 1924 (the year after reorganization) (R. 521)   57.860%

Apportionment per cent decrease due to removal of business and property (R. 521) 29.695%

1924 apportionable income (Exh. C-2 (c) Audit Report) (R. 521) $2,240,038.35

Apportionment per cent decrease due to removal of business and property..   29.695%

Reduction in income apportioned to Wisconsin due to 29.695% decrease in apportionment percentage $665,179.39

Interest and dividends received by Palmolive Company (Delaware) following residence outside the state (R. 521)   60,507.92

1924 income recognized by the Tax Commission as non-taxable due to removal
of business and property from state   725,687.31

"The above computation shows the reduction in percentage and income for the year 1924, and the following computation shows the average reduction in percentage and income for the three years following the
reorganization as compared with the three years preceding the reorganization:

Average apportionable income for first
three years following reorganization
(R. 521) $2,428,548.83
Average apportionment percentage decrease due to removal of business and
property 33.751%
Average reduction in income apportioned
to Wisconsin due to 33.751% decrease
in average apportionment percentage $819,659.51
Average amount of interest and dividends
treated as outside income (R. 521)..   96,660.84
Average income 1924–1926, recognized by
the Tax Commission as non-taxable
due to removal of business and property from the state 916,320.35

"It is apparent from the above schedule that the removal of property and business from the state had a
very substantial effect upon the income taxable in Wisconsin, and the Commission has recognized in the assessment that a large amount of income was legiti-
mately removed from the state of Wisconsin through
the removal of property and business as a result of the
reorganization. It cannot be said, therefore, that the
Tax Commission has attempted to tax income from
such property as was removed from the state. Not con-
tent with such reduction in taxable income for Wisconsin as would result under Section 71.02 of the statutes
from the actual removal of property and business from
the state, the appellant taxpayer apparently sought by

a carefully designed plan to create affiliated corporations with which contracts and arrangements might be
made for the very purpose of determining the income
to be taxed by the state of Wisconsin. After a careful
consideration of the original contracts and arrangements entered into between the several corporations at
the time of the reorganization and as amended since
that time, it would be unreasonable to say, in adopting
their plan of reorganization, its effect upon income
taxation in Wisconsin was not definitely in the minds
of the appellants' officials.''

The apportionment of the combined income of the four
companies was used only for the purpose of determining
the income properly assignable to Wisconsin because in the
judgment of the Tax Commission the income assigned to
Wisconsin by taxpayer's method of separate accounting under the intercompany contracts and intercompany arrangements does not reasonably reflect the income properly assignable to Wisconsin. By this method the Commission
determined the income or profit derived from business
transacted and properly located in Wisconsin for income
tax purposes.

It is true that the group of corporations is made up of
four legal entities which are fully recognized by the Commission. It is also true that the amount of actual income
derived from business transacted and property located
within the state has not been properly reported by those
members of the four corporations that were assigned to
carry on the operations within the state. On the other
hand, the income reported by these members of the group
was derived from the contracts and intercompany arrangements existing between the inter-related corporations but
which in fact are doing business practically as one. *In
other words, the income assignable to Wisconsin according
to petitioner's method is an artificial income which might
have been fixed at any figure the common officers of these*

companies saw fit to fix. It is not income reflected from ordinary business operations in an economic sense, that is, as affected by the economic laws governing the price of materials, labor and market value of finished products, etc. It is reasonable to say that the legislature under the income tax law has sought to tax income from business operations as determined by economic conditions and economic laws. The income assigned to Wisconsin by this corporate group does not result from the operation of such various economic forces. The Tax Commission has found that the contracts of 1924 and 1925 are not fair and result in an unfair return on the business and property of the petitioner, done and located in Wisconsin. The operating contract of 1924 produces a strikingly different result from the operating contract of 1925. In the operation of both contracts the effect of economic forces has been almost entirely excluded and the parties have attempted to stipulate and fix the income which they desire to assign to Wisconsin.

The Tax Commission has assigned to Wisconsin an income which it finds to be the proper and reasonable income from the business and property of the Wisconsin corporation growing out of its Wisconsin operations only. The petitioner, on the other hand, attempts to fix the income assignable to Wisconsin by means of operating contracts of its own manufacture. Where the petitioner claims the line can be drawn with reference to such contracts is difficult to understand. In a court of equity which of these methods is most equitable? Is the finding of the Tax Commission, charged with a public duty of collecting revenue for the state, to be disturbed without the most clear and satisfactory proof?

"Of necessity the details of the administration of the income tax laws must be left to the determination of the Tax Commission and its staff who possess expert knowledge with reference to the problems of taxation which is not possessed either by the legislature or the court. So long as the Commission does not tax as income that which is in fact not income for taxation purposes, the Commission must be given a large degree of discretion *in determining the method that will be adopted in ascertaining the taxable income of any income taxpayer.*"

> *Motor Acceptance Co. vs. Tax Commission*, 193 Wis. 41 at 46.

In the same case the court says:

> "Undoubtedly no system of taxation will be devised that will do absolute justice to every taxpayer. All that can be done is to adopt the system or method that will most clearly reflect the taxable income."

The Commission proceeded under section 71.25 (2) of the Wisconsin statutes and the general authority inherent in the Tax Commission independent of such statute, to determine the true Wisconsin income of the Wisconsin Company.

> *Cliffs Chemical Co. vs. Wisconsin Tax Commission*, 193 Wis. 295, 277 U. S. 574.

This case has no analogy to the Studebaker case in which the Tax Commission of the state of New York attempted to assess the whole profit to the subsidiary and nothing to the parent. The court says in that case:

> "The business transacted by the principal included the process of manufacture carried on in Michigan and Indiana, a process which was anterior of necessity to any service by the agent. We find no basis for holding that a fair agreement between the parent which manufactured and the subsidiary which sold would have given *the whole profit* to the subsidiary and nothing to the parent."

> *People ex rel. Studebaker Corp. vs. Gilchrist* 244 N. Y. 114 at 122.

In the same case the court says, affirming expressly the proceeding of the Wisconsin Tax Commission:

"We assume once again that the taxing officers of the state may disregard a subsidiary altogether as a bookkeeping device when there is evidence to justify the finding that it is that device and nothing more. In that event there is power to tax the parent corporation, the owner of the stock, on the basis of the consolidated income apportioned to New York."

People ex rel. Studebaker Corp. vs. Gilchrist,
244 N. Y. 114.

There is a strong dissenting opinion in this case by two of the judges. In this dissenting opinion, Judge Crane says:

"To arrive at such a conclusion, the Tax Commission could adopt and use any information it had and this is specifically stated. It did use the figures given by the relator and the process of allocation which was the correct method for ascertaining profit when a foreign corporation was doing business directly. In the absence of other information furnished by the relator, this, in my judgment, was legal and proper." Page 131.

In a recent Massachusetts case, a foreign corporation doing business in the state of Massachusetts, soliciting transportation in less than car load lots, stored the goods and did the carting in Boston free of charge. When it accumulated a car load of goods it shipped the same in car load lots. The company so manipulated its books that it made no profit out of the carting and storing of the goods in Massachusetts but claimed to have made its profit entirely upon the rate which it got in car load lots, which profit it claimed to be exempt as interstate business. The income tax law of Massachusetts taxes corporations on the basis of the portion of its property fairly attributable to

Massachusetts business.   The Massachusetts court in dealing with this case, says:

> "In our opinion the circumstances that the petitioner
> makes no profit out of its Massachusetts business,
> charging only its actual disbursements in this connec-
> tion, is immaterial.   There is no pretence that the pe-
> titioner is an eleemosynary corporation doing this
> work for purely altruistic aims.   It is a business cor-
> poration organized for profit.   It cannot avoid respon-
> sibility to local laws for local business by so gauging
> its business as to allocate its profits wholly to inter-
> state business.   It has adopted this method voluntarily
> for its own ends.   The commonwealth is not bound by
> these methods.   The taxing power has a right to look
> to the substance of things and collect its imposts from
> whatever is within the jurisdiction of its constitutional
> laws."
>
> *Judson Freight Forwarding Co. vs. Common-*
> *wealth*, 242 Mass. 47, 136 N. E. 375 at 380.

Courts have uniformly gone behind devices such as that
employed in this case in order to compel a corporation to
pay its just income taxes.   There are numerous cases in the
courts where corporations have leased property under an
agreement with the lessee that the rents are to be paid
directly to the stockholders.   The courts in such cases have
subjected the corporations to income taxes and have not
upheld their claims that they are without income.

> *Rensselaer vs. Irwin*, 239 Fed. 739.
> *Rennselaer vs. Irwin*, 249 Fed. 726.
> *West & Strong Ry. vs. Malley*, 246 Fed. 625.
> *Houston Belt Ry. vs. United States* 250 Fed. 1.

Courts readily go behind the corporate form in cases
such as that herein considered and look to the real relationship of the parties even without the assistance of any statute.   As stated in a recent case:

"The railroad companies contended that the Minneapolis Eastern Railway Company was a separate entity and that the ownership of stock by the railroad companies did not create the relationship of principal and agent. As to this the Supreme Court said: 'While the statements of the law thus relied upon are satisfactory in the connection in which they were used, they have been plainly and repeatedly held not applicable where stock ownership has been resorted to, not for the purpose of participating in the affairs of a corporation in the nominal and usual manner, but for the purpose, as in this case, of controlling a subsidiary company so that it may be used as a mere agency or instrumentality of the owning company or companies. * * *' In such a case the courts will not permit themselves to be blinded or deceived by mere forms or law but, regardless of fictions, *will deal with a substance of the transaction involved as if the corporate agency did not exist and as the justice of the case may require.*"

> *Wabash Ry. Co. vs. American Refrigerator Transit Co.*, 7 Fed (2) 335 at 344 and cases cited.

The courts are not obliged to accept the contracts and arrangements of the petitioner simply because they are in form between separate entities. The courts are free to go behind such entities to discover devices to evade taxation or to evade any other public duty or public obligation.

"That the state from whose laws property and business and industry derive the protection and security without which production and gainful occupation would be impossible, is debarred from exacting a share of those gains in the form of income taxes for the support of the government, is a proposition so wholly inconsistent with fundamental principles as to be refuted by its mere statement. That it may tax the land but not the crop, the tree but not the fruit, the mine or well but not the product, the business but not the profit derived from it, is wholly inadmissible.

"The rights of the several states to exercise the widest liberty with respect to the imposition of internal taxes always has been recognized in the decisions of this court. In *McCulloch vs. Maryland,* 4 Wheat. 316, while denying their power to impose a tax upon any of the operations of the federal government, Mr. Chief Justice Marshall, speaking for the court, conceded that the states have full power to tax their own people and their own property, and also that the power is not confined to the people and property of a state but may be exercised upon every object brought within its jurisdiction; saying, 'It is obvious that it is an incident of sovereignty and is co-extensive with that to which it is an incident. All subjects over which the sovereign power of a state extends are objects of taxation'."

Shaffer vs. Carter, 252 U. S. 37 at 50 and 51, 64
Law Ed. 445.

"We have had frequent occasion to consider questions of state taxation in the light of the federal constitution and the scope and limits of national interference are well settled. There is no general supervision on the part of the nation over state taxation and in respect to the latter the state has, speaking generally, the freedom of a sovereign both as to the objects and methods."

Michigan Central R. R. Co. vs. Powers 201 U. S.
245 at 292.
State Tax on Foreign-held Bonds, 15 Wall. 300.

"And we deem it clear, upon principal as well as authority, that just as a state may impose general income taxes upon its own citizens and residents whose persons are subject to its control, it may, as a necessary consequence, levy a duty of like character and not more onerous in its effect, upon incomes accruing to non-residents from their property or business within the state, or their occupations carried on therein; enforcing payment so far as it can by the exercise of a just control over persons and property within its borders."

Shaffer vs. Carter Id. page 52.

"The fact that it required the personal skill and management of appellant to bring his income from producing property in Oklahoma to fruition and that his management was exerted from his place of business in another state, did not deprive Oklahoma of jurisdiction to tax the income which arose within its own borders. The personal element cannot, by any fiction, oust the jurisdiction of the state within which the income actually arises, and whose authority over it operates in rem."

Shaffer vs. Carter, Id. page 55.

The operations of the petitioning company and its subsidiary, the Wisconsin Company, were subject to the jurisdiction of the state of Wisconsin, and it was proper and constitutional for the Tax Commission to reach the proper income of the Wisconsin Company.

Underwood Typewriter Co. vs. Chamberlain, 254 U. S. 113, 65 Law Ed. 165.

Petitioner is in error in claiming that the Circuit Court failed to properly interpret and follow the case of Hans Rees' Sons recently decided by this Court and that such case, in any way forbids a state from apportioning taxes to the state under the circumstances followed in this case. In the Hans Rees' Sons case, the evidence showed without dispute that during the tax years in question, the percentage of income earned in North Carolina by the company did not in any event exceed 21.7%, (Page 134) while the amount allocated by the taxing authorities to North Carolina was approximately 80%. The court in considering the case fully affirmed the rule in *Underwood Typewriter Co. vs. Chamberlain*, 254 U. S. 113, *Bass, Ratcliff & Gretton, Ltd. vs. State Tax Commission*, 266 U. S. 271, and *National Leather Co. vs. Massachusetts*, 277 U. S. 413. The court quotes in the Hans Rees Case from the Underwood case and calls attention to the following quotation from that case:

"There is consequently nothing in this record to show that the method of apportionment adopted by the state was inherently arbitrary or that its application to this corporation produced an unreasonable result."

Neither is there any evidence produced by petitioner in this case that the Wisconsin Tax Commission's method of apportionment was inherently arbitrary or that its application to the Palmolive Company produced an unreasonable result. On the contrary, the petitioner stubbornly insisted and still insists that the fictitious contracts in question reflected the true Wisconsin income and that the Tax Commission had no right to consider any other income no matter how apparent. Evidence is wholly lacking in the record of any facts or figures produced by the petitioner to show the true amount of income apportionable to Wisconsin from the business of the combined companies differed from that found by the Tax Commission. The court in the Hans Rees' Sons case quotes with approval the following language from the Bass, Ratcliff & Gretton case:

"So in the present case we are of the opinion that as the company carried on the unitary business of manufacturing and selling ale, in which its profits were earned by a series of transactions beginning with the manufacture in England and ending in sales in New York and other places—the process of manufacturing resulting in no profits until it ends in sales—the state was justified in attributing to New York a just proportion of the profits earned by the company *from the unitary business*. Nor do we find that the method of apportioning the net income on the basis of the ratio of the segregated assets located in New York and elsewhere was inherently arbitrary or a mere effort to reach profits earned elsewhere under the guise of legitimate taxation. *It is not shown in the present case any more than in the Underwood case that this application of the statutory method of apportionment has produced an unreasonable result.*" P. 131.

"Generally speaking, strict mathematical certainty cannot reasonably be expected in such matters. In the routine of taxation as applied to ordinary business, slight departures either in method or computation involving trivial amounts will not be noticed. Having in mind the magnitude of the business here involved, we believe the commission reached a conclusion which sufficiently approximates justice between this taxpayer and the state as to require approval of the result."

Decision of Judge Alschuler in this case.
(R. 618)
Buick Motor Co. vs. City of Milwaukee, et al.,
48 F. (2) 801.

The Hans Rees' Sons case was decided wholly upon the ground that the court found:

"Evidence which was found to be lacking in the Underwood and Bass cases is present here. These decisions are not authority for the conclusion that where a corporation manufactures in one state and sells in another, the net profits of the *entire transaction* as a unitary enterprise may be attributed regardless of evidence, to either state. In the Underwood case, it was not decided that *the entire net profits* of the total business were to be allocated to Connecticut because that was the place of manufacture, or in the Bass case that the *entire net profits* were to be allocated to New York because that was the place where sales were made. In both instances a method of apportionment was involved which, as was said in the Underwood case, for all that appears in the record, reached and was meant to reach only the profits earned within the state. The difficulty with the evidence offered in the Underwood case was that it failed to establish that the amount of net income which the corporation was charged in Connecticut under the method adopted was not reasonably attributable to the processes conducted within the borders of that state; and in the Bass case the court found a similar defect in proof with respect to transactions in New York."

Hans Rees' Sons vs. North Carolina, 283 U. S. 132–133.

We submit that there is a similar defect in the evidence in this case. Petitioner made no effort to show that the apportionment of income to Wisconsin was arbitrary or unreasonable except to rely upon the contracts.

The court further says in the Hans Rees' Sons case:

"Undoubtedly, the enterprise of a corporation which manufactures and sells its manufactured products *is ordinarily a unitary business* and all the factors in that enterprise are essential to the realization of profits. The difficulty of making an exact apportionment is apparent and hence when the state has adopted a method not *intrinsically arbitrary* it will be sustained *until proof is offered of an unreasonable and arbitrary application in particular cases:*" (page 133)

The business is just as much unitary when carried on by different corporations acting together as a unit.

The accountant who examined the books of the appellant testified that it was impossible to determine the correct income of any of the affiliated companies by a separate accounting. (R. 79–80)

The apportionment made by the Wisconsin Tax Commission should be sustained unless there is proof that it is "*unreasonable and arbitrary,*" it not being "*intrinsically arbitrary.*" The Hans Rees' Sons decision puts the burden upon the petitioner to make such proof and this the petitioner failed to meet.

The court in the Hans Rees' Sons Case recognizes the well established rule that the presumption is in favor of the taxing officers and that the burden rests upon the one attacking their acts to show that the acts are unreasonable, unjust or arbitrary or violate some constitutional right of the attacking party. Such is the law universally recognized.

"The good faith of such officers and the validity of their actions are presumed; when assailed the burden of proof is upon the complaining party."

> *Sunday Lake Iron Co. vs. Wakefield*, 247 U. S. 350 at 353, and numerous cases cited therein.

The Hans Rees' Sons case also reaffirms the holding in the case of *National Leather Company vs. Massachusetts*, 277 U. S. 413 as well as the Underwood and Bass cases, and in no way condemns the principles of apportionment followed by the Wisconsin Tax Commission. The evidence in the Hans Rees' Sons case was definite and positive as to the proportion of the business attributable to North Carolina and the taxing authorities of North Carolina ignored such evidence and attempted to tax four times that amount to that state. It was solely upon this ground that the Hans Rees' Sons case condemned the North Carolina tax.

The case at bar is not brought within the principles laid down in the Rees case. There was no attempt in this case to show that the amount of income attributable to Wisconsin was different from what the Tax Commission found other than to rely upon the fictitious inter-company contracts. There is no attempt to show that the findings of the Wisconsin Tax Commission work any injustice to the petitioner or that the findings are arbitrary or unreasonable. As said in the Underwood case where the percentage of income attributed to Connecticut was forty-seven per cent,

"For aught that appears the percentage of net profits earned in Connecticut may have been much larger than forty-seven per cent."

For aught that appears in this case, the percentage attributable to Wisconsin might have been much larger than the Tax Commission found. The petitioner has not met the burden of proof resting upon it by showing the contrary.

This is a suit in equity and it is incumbent upon the petitioner to show that it has been inequitably dealt with. This it has utterly failed to show.

VII

CONCLUSION

We submit that this court in cases almost on all fours with the one at bar has already said that there is no substantial federal question presented by the record.

 Cliffs Chemical Company vs. Wisconsin Tax Commission, 277 U. S. 574.

 Buick Motor Company vs. City of Milwaukee et al., — U. S. —.

In these cases this court denied a writ of certiorari to the Circuit Court of Appeals.

The income of citizens of the state is undeniably within the jurisdiction of the state to tax. The constitutionality and construction of the state laws *enacted within that jurisdiction*—the determination of what is income under the law, the methods of ascertaining it, the classes of citizens and incomes so taxed, and the procedure in levying and collecting the tax—are questions of local law only. The judgment in this case proceeded solely upon the state law, which is adequate to dispose of the case without reaching any federal question; and, although violation of the due process and equal protection of the law clauses of the fourteenth amendment in the application of the state law to the assessment of petitioner's income is, in form, claimed, such claim seems clearly without color or substance, and the judgment is therefore not open to review here.

 French vs. Taylor, 199 U. S. 274.

 Elder vs. Wood, 208 U. S. 226.

Hodge vs. Muscatine County, 196 U. S. 276.

Green vs. Frazier, 253 U. S. 233.

Nickel vs. Cole, 256 U. S. 222.

Baker vs. Druesedow, 263 U. S. 137.

St. Joseph etc. R. Co. vs. Steele, 167 U. S. 659.

Proctor & Gamble Distributing Company vs. Sherman, 2 F. (2) 165.

Shaffer vs. Carter, 252 U. S. 37.

Michigan Central R. R. Co. vs. Powers, 201 U. S. 245.

State Tax on Foreign-held Bonds, 15 Wall. 300.

Underwood Typewriter Co. vs. Chamberlain, 254 U. S. 113, 65 L. Ed. 165.

Judson Freight Forwarding Co. vs. Commonwealth, 242 Mass. 47, 136 N. E. 375.

Upon the authority of the Hans Rees' Sons case alone the decision of the learned trial judge affirmed by the Court of Appeals should be sustained.

We respectfully submit that the petition for a writ of certiorari in this case should be denied.

Respectfully submitted,

JOHN W. REYNOLDS,
Attorney General of Wisconsin,

THEO. W. BRAZEAU,
Special Counsel for
Wisconsin Tax Commission,

LEO J. FEDERER,
Counsel for Respondents.

Lightning Source UK Ltd.
Milton Keynes UK
UKOW04f0602040417

298299UK00009B/382/P